DATE D

PUBLIC EDUCATION

Public Education

WHO'S IN CHARGE?

Fred G. Burke

 PRAEGER

New York
Westport, Connecticut
London

Library of Congress Cataloging-in-Publication Data

Burke, Fred G.
  Public education : who's in charge? / Fred G. Burke.
    p.   cm.
  Includes bibliographical references.
  ISBN 0-275-93402-0 (alk. paper)
    1. Education and state—United States. 2. Public schools—United
States. 3. Youth—Government policy—United States. I. Title.
LC89.B87   1990
379.73—dc20   89-38008

Library of Congress Catalog Card Number: 89-38008
ISBN: 0-275-93402-0

First published in 1990

Praeger Publishers, One Madison Avenue, New York, NY 10010
A division of Greenwood Press, Inc.

Printed in the United States of America

The paper used in this book complies with the
Permanent Paper Standard issued by the National
Information Standards Organization (Z39.48-1984).

10 9 8 7 6 5 4 3 2 1

For "Carol," which in this vernacular translates: "infinite patience and extraordinary empathy"

Contents

Preface

As commissioner of education first in Rhode Island and then in New Jersey for some dozen years, I had a long and unique opportunity to experience the difficulty of bringing about a minimal level of educational uniformity and standards in the face of a tradition of local control and a determination to perceive of education almost solely in parochial terms. If the United States is to develop "public" policies capable of addressing a "national" crisis, it is imperative that consideration be given to alternative policy processes. However, as long as the dialogue is dominated by an educational establishment and an academic community deeply imbued with the lore and mystic of exclusively local control of education, it is not likely that alternative policy processes will receive serious consideration.

The possibility of contemplating a public educational policy for the entire nation is also problematically difficult for an additional reason: the gradual evolution of a nonpublic process for making national educational policy. This uniquely American phenomenon, which I have termed "para-private," has evolved in response to the absence of a national public educational policy process, an attribute characteristic of all major nations. The tendency for the participants in this private network of individuals and institutions to belong to the educational establishment and therefore to subscribe to the inviolate virtues of local control of education, and to a shared suspicion of state and/or federal involvement, also makes it unlikely that this para-private process will bring about significant changes in the existing parochial policy process.

These thoughts are the source of my concern and anxiety—a fear that the nation is on the brink of calamity, in part because of its failure to comprehend or, if it does comprehend, because of its failure to address the true dimensions of the plight of its children and youth. Attempting to avert catastrophe by making only marginal changes and adjustments in the existing system is but a guarantee of an impending apocalypse.

This volume, drawing on many years of personal experience and, perhaps more important, a contemplation of that experience, is an attempt to focus attention on these concerns, with the hope that their perusal will contribute to a greater willingness to contemplate policy alternatives more boldly. What we think and write are frequently shaped by our experiences. Perhaps if I share a slightly edited version of an actual event, the reader might gain better insight as to where this book is coming from.

In 1970, while commissioner of education in Rhode Island, I was told that I was about to be "marched on" by a group of predominantly black and Hispanic mothers. The reason for their discontent was the precipitous preclusion of children's clothing as a part of the Title I entitlement. Title I of the U.S. Elementary and Secondary Education Act was the major federal educational program targeted to disadvantaged children. The hundred or so angry mothers, many of whom were members of a federally required Title I Parents Advisory Council, had already marched on the Providence school superintendent's office. There they were told, I suspect with obvious relief, that they had come to the wrong place. They were informed that the source of the problem was with the state commissioner. By the time the ladies arrived at the Rhode Island Department of Education they were even more angry, for they perceptively sensed they were getting the runaround.

The leader of the group, clearly not a person to be trifled with lightly, demanded of the commissioner, "Who in hell is in charge around here?" And that is essentially the subject of this book! The federal government, for reasons examined in detail in subsequent chapters, has a minor but important role to play in education and related child and youth services. Day-to-day education is provided by local schools as largely determined by local school boards. Thus, the coterie of angry mothers was correct to march on the Providence school superintendent, for it was he and his principals who made the clothing available. The concerned ladies were also correct to proceed up the hill to the state commissioner's office when they received no satisfaction. Who is in charge? I tried to explain that the money for the clothes came from Washington but that there was no law requiring that their children had to be provided with clothing. Indeed, Rhode Island could choose not to participate in Title I, but this would mean forgoing millions of dollars of federal funds.

"Who said that we could use these monies for clothing and now says we can't?" Simple enough question, but how does one answer without seeming to be passing the buck? The U.S. government, in deference to tradition, does not get involved in business-making decisions about public schools and schooling; this is the prerogative of the states, who in turn delegate most of their responsibilities to relatively autonomous local school systems.

"Then why were funds from Washington used to buy children's clothing last week but not this week?" Well a number of faceless bureaucrats, far enough removed from Rhode Island to be spared the wrath of angry mothers, decided that Rhode Island's decision to spend some of its Title I money for clothing for your children was not what Congress intended. "Why was it okay last week but not this week?" Somebody in Washington changed his or her mind. "I still don't know who in hell is in charge, and frankly we really don't give a damn so long as our children have clothes so they can go to school!"

The education of the nation's children—and seeing that they do not go hungry and that they are not denied shelter or adequate clothing—is today acknowledged to be a national concern worthy of a national policy and appropriate legislation. However, when it comes to schools and schooling, there is no national policy; from a national perspective and from the point of view of a hundred angry Providence mothers, nobody is in charge—and that is the problem. And that is what this book is all about.

Many persons, some unaware, have contributed to this book in a variety of important ways, for writing about education is itself a constant learning process. I am particularly indebted to my wife Carol Sterling Burke, who critically read every version of every chapter. My good friend Ken Auletta read and critiqued an early version of the manuscript, as did my colleague Everett Ladd. Their suggestions were very useful, and I am most grateful. I would also like to express my appreciation to the University of Connecticut Research Foundation, which awarded me a grant that facilitated the research. And I would like to acknowledge the assistance of Carol Steen, a super graduate student at the University of Connecticut, who helped with the research, notes, and bibliography.

1

A Nation at Risk

Is it possible that the great education reform era of the 1980s has already come and gone? The numerous commissions and reports, summarized in some detail below, have not culminated in significant changes in the nation's educational systems or processes. Were this simply a case of failed reform, we might dismiss the efforts as well intended but longer on rhetoric than results. However, the implications of a decade of debate documenting the colossal failure of the nation's schools to prepare America's youth for what the authors of the reform studies agreed will be a most problematic and challenging future constitute a far more serious matter.

Educational reform movements occur periodically, usually in response to a real or perceived national crisis that, at least in part, can be attributed to the failures of public education. Because there are few, if any, domestic or foreign crises that cannot somehow be related to the condition of public education, and because the schools and their clientele pose an attractive and relatively safe target for national discontent, the attribution of the country's relative economic decline to the seemingly related poor educational performance of its youth is not surprising.

The seemingly endless and monotonously similar spate of studies and reports analyzing, documenting, and proposing to remedy the educational malaise leaves this writer with a gnawing unease and with a conviction that the educational reform process may have left us worse off than we were before. I say this because two decades of intensive, sometimes difficult, but always interesting involvement in public education has convinced me that for both advertent and inadvertent reasons we consistently have posed the wrong fundamental questions and therefore not only have generated the wrong answers but have led many to believe that things are getting better.

The national crisis is not simply that of the quality of public education but, more profoundly, the emergence of a rapidly growing population of alienated, relatively little educated, predominantly black and Hispanic youth, who increasingly constitute a distinct, isolated subculture. Although this is in part an education phenomenon, an insistence on perceiving it as but an integral aspect of needed reforms in the nation's schools and schooling tends to misread the essence of this crisis and thus contributes to a failure to appreciate its critical dimensions and real significance.

For the most part the debate and ensuing reform proposals have been cast in education—in school and schooling terms—because those who make up the reform forum are drawn predominantly from the ranks of the educational establishment and related institutions. It is only recently that a few major studies and reform proposals targeted on the plight of predominantly minority, culturally and economically disadvantaged children and youth have surfaced.

Because the dialogue has been dominated by the educational establishment and has concentrated on schools and schooling, the recommendations look to the nation's educational systems as instruments for bringing about the proposed changes. Thus, we are asked to put our faith in the deliberations and resultant policies of some 16,000 semiautonomous school districts and fifty widely

differing state governments somehow miraculously to address
what is uniformly acknowledged to be a national crisis.

No governance prerogatives in America are as decentralized or
as passionately defended as those that characterize educational
decision making and administration. To expect that this near state
of educational anarchy will somehow steep itself in the plethora
of reform proposals and in a miraculous fashion combine thousands of parochial decisions into an effective and sufficiently
uniform educational policy to address successfully the nation's
critical education and youth policy is a dangerous denial of reality.

The National Commission on Excellence in Education, in its
most influential and frequently quoted study, concluded that the
nation was at risk. Indeed, the report warns that the nation's "once
unchallenged preeminence in commerce and industry, science and
technological innovation" has fallen prey to our global competitors. Also perceived to be at risk was the nation's "prosperity,
security, and civility."[1] The tone of this much acclaimed document
strongly conveys the view that both at home and abroad the nation
surely is flirting with disaster. To what foreign plot or domestic
deviance can one attribute this impending tragedy? The commission concludes that a goodly portion of the responsibility is attributable to a "rising tide of mediocrity" that it believes is dangerously
eroding the "educational foundations of our society."

Although *A Nation at Risk* is attributed to many aspects of
America's changing culture and society, the commission speaks
first at length about the country's deteriorating economic position
in an increasingly competitive world. Although it is the NATION
that is perceived to be dangerously at risk—in important part
because of the eroding quality of education—no national remedies
are advanced. The reports are limited to pleas to 16,000 semiautonomous school districts, to somehow address the national crisis.

If indeed the nation is at risk, it seems logical and appropriate
to ask, What is the nation doing to address this impending catastrophe? Were a crisis of this magnitude and consequence to afflict
a public policy arena other than education, one would anticipate
that relevant congressional committees would schedule hearings,

order commission reports, and draft appropriate legislation and that the executive branch would propose its own legislative remedies. But when the crisis is about the education of the nation's youth, we are not inclined to turn to the political and governmental processes employed for most other occasions of national crisis but rather to a policy process composed of an overlapping network of private foundations, selective universities, and academics—a process studied in some detail in Chapter 3.

The past decade has witnessed a plethora of studies designed to ascertain the dimensions of the crisis in education and to advance appropriate policy solutions. But as long as such commissions are not constituted as an integral part of the political/governmental policy process, it is unlikely, regardless of the sponsoring agency, that recommendations will ultimately translate into authoritative public policy.

A brief review of selected aspects of a few of the various educational reform proposals advanced over the past decade is presented below to set the stage for a critical analysis of the unintended but dire consequences of this peculiarly American way of making fundamental educational decisions.

REFORM PROCESS AND PROPOSALS

The National Commission, appointed in 1982 by President Ronald Reagan on the advice of the secretary of education, Terrel Bell, included a proper sprinkling of teachers, educational administrators, labor leaders, university professors and presidents, and corporate representatives.[2] This august commission was chaired by David Gardner, president elect of the University of Utah, an educational leader who has contributed significantly to efforts at educational reform over the past two decades.

Between 1982 and 1987 more than ten important studies of the serious educational problems besieging the nation, replete with proposed remedies, have been entered into the current educational dialogue.[3] Unfortunately, this plethora of studies and recommendations is less distinguished by its creativity and variation than by a striking degree of similarity of analysis and proposed remediation.[4] Graham Down, president of the Council for Basic Education, not only questions the relevance of the many reform studies and proposals but shares this writer's view that they even may be dysfunctional. "These reports, with their numbing similarity to all the reports generated by high level education commissions over the last thirty years, may have already become an inadvertent impediment to educational improvement."[5]

Two interrelated issues afflicting contemporary American society are highlighted by the many studies as correlating closely with the erosion of educational performance. The decline in student performance over the past three decades, as determined by a variety of essentially "test" measures, is portrayed as a major contributor to the nation's increasingly precarious hold on the top rung of global preeminence. Although the studies differ somewhat in emphasis, they tend to agree that a major culprit is an increasingly vacuous curriculum, spawned by the educational progressivism of the tumultuous 1960s. The major studies, although differing somewhat as to how, agree that the curriculum needs tightening up, with more time devoted to the "basics"—math, science, and language. The National Commission on Excellence boldly advances what it terms the "Five New Basics," which on close examination suspiciously resemble the old basics, for example, four years of English, three years of math, three years of science, three years of social studies, and one-half year of computer science.

Despite unanimity as to the crisis nature of the deterioration in the quality of the nation's educational record, the many studies seem studiously to avoid advancing new and bold ideas. There are a few exceptions. *High School: A Report on Secondary Education in America*, chaired by Ernest Boyer, president of the Carnegie Foundation for the Advancement of Teaching, in addition to the usual concern with curriculum and an emphasis on the basics, also recommends a required course in "Community Service." However, with very few exceptions the hundreds of recommendations differ only slightly—and mostly in emphasis. Indeed, they differ hardly at all from the many recommendations that have been made by study groups and commissions over the past half century.

The fact that a disproportionate number of the studies are concerned almost exclusively with secondary education reflects the general consensus that it is here that the problem is most crucial and acute. Also, there is slight awareness that the crisis not only is associated with the nation's secondary schools but is found in its most virulent form to afflict minority children in depressed rural and urban areas. However, with rare exception, most of the reports (until the late 1980s) avoid dealing with this sensitive and controversial phenomenon. The near unanimous demand for more rigorous curriculum, promotion, and graduation standards—standards that most students in the nation's inner cities and rural slums already do not meet—in the face of the 50 percent drop-out rate is suggestive of a disinclination to confront directly the more fundamental issue of a minority youth in crisis.

While these generalizations essentially describe the many studies carried out in the early 1980s, more recently a number of efforts addressing the broader and more fundamental issues of a generation of youth at crisis have been published.[6]

LIMITATIONS OF THE
EDUCATION REFORM STUDIES

The preoccupation with deteriorating school performance, as measured by standardized test scores, as the root cause of *A Nation At Risk* acts to obscure the more fundamental issue of a more general malaise afflicting disproportionately urban youth—one that has the potential of calcifying a permanent underclass.

Although test scores, by and large, have fallen across the board, this condition is most pronounced and acute among poor urban and rural youth—the nation's most rapidly growing population and one that is increasingly black and Hispanic. Even when the many reform studies reveal an awareness of the peculiarly urban and minority nature of the crisis, there is a disappointing dearth of proposals directed specifically to this population. It is as if the problem of poor urban and rural children and youth is but a regional aspect of the overall national educational problem. Therefore, it is assumed that the general remedies proposed, with possibly a bit more of this and that, here and there, should suffice. It is highly unlikely, however, that the orthodoxy of higher standards, improved teaching and better teachers, higher and differential salaries, merit pay, extended school day and school year, less bureaucracy, more teacher and school autonomy, and so on, will contribute very much to resolving the deepening plight of the nation's needy children and troubled youth.

Most of the recommendations suggest an improved process for policy-making at the school and district levels, to be achieved, for example, by the systematic setting of goals and objectives, decentralization of policy to teachers, and by frequent assessment and evaluation. In reality there is little new here, for beginning in the 1970s many states began to require local districts and schools to develop and implement such rational planning models. New Jersey's often-cited 1975 Thorough and Efficient Education Law, with which this writer was intimately involved for some eight years, provided for a policy process emphasizing the setting of goals and an accompanying accountability structure.

The plethora of reform recommendations also tends to agree that the time spent in the classroom-learning mode is too brief and not well organized. Reflected in most studies is a concern with the division of the school day and year by subject matter and time. The proposed remedies are similar to those that most educators have heard advanced for the past three decades, for example, extended school year and/or school day, the addition or deletion of specific activities or subjects, more or less out-of-school study and homework, more emphasis on analytical and reasoning skills and less on rote memory, more student and teacher mentoring, and so on.

The major studies devote considerable attention to classroom structure and management as critically affecting educational performance. But here, too, the recommendations are surprisingly similar and mundane. Despite the seemingly obvious relationship between declining educational outcomes and a uniquely parochial educational system, the reform proposals carefully avoid suggesting significant changes in the intergovernmental allocation of authority and responsibility. The shibboleths "local control," "states' rights," and "fear of federal control" are alive and well. A number of reform proposals advanced in 1988 and 1989, by both the National Education Association (NEA) and the American Federation of Teachers (AFT), as well as by a number of respected educational writers, advocate more—not less—decentralization of authority for educational decision making, arguing that the solution to the crisis lies in turning the management and activities of the schools over to the teachers, parents, and community at the building level.

Ours is the only nation in which fundamental decisions concerning what is taught, by whom, to what end, at whose expense, and where are essentially made by some fifty states and 16,000 relatively autonomous school districts, aided and abetted by an equivalent number of teacher and administrator unions. Despite mounting evidence that the inadequacies of a highly decentralized educational policy process are in large part responsible for a nation at risk, the one recommendation not forthcoming was a proposal for even minor changes in the manner in which the nation's decentralized and federal structure governs and manages its educational enterprise. No proposals were advanced that would in effect consolidate, or even marginally centralize, educational policy-making in response to a premise that the existing parochial system is partly responsible for the crisis. One looks in vain for imaginative suggestions proposing alterations in the traditional sharing of authority and responsibility among the national governmental institutions and those at the state, local, and community levels.

AVOIDANCE OF STRUCTURAL REFORM

It is significant and revealing that only about half of the many studies offer any recommendations concerning even minor alterations in the role of the federal government. If the nation is truly at risk, as the reports trumpet, and in significant part because of the inadequacy of the current anarchic process for making and implementing educational policy, a failure to address the fundamental issue of who makes what educational policy seems to be either a gross or a convenient oversight.

In those rare instances where the reports do suggest that there is a role for the federal government in educational reform, care is taken to limit its activities to such traditionally limited assignments as data gathering, research, special assistance for special populations, teacher support, and constitutional and other civil rights of students and educators.

The evolution of the nation's unique system of educational governance is treated in some detail in Chapter 2. At this point it is sufficient to advance the argument that the deeply ingrained values associated with local control and the perceived constitutional limitations on a significant federal role in educational policy-making, in important part, are responsible for the absence of imaginative and bold reform recommendations commensurate with the dramatically portrayed magnitude of the nation's risk. The persistence of a nineteenth-century parochial policy process, as the nation approaches the threshold of the twenty-first century, also is responsible for the disinclination of the many commissions (with the exceptions noted) to look beyond "education" and "school" and to attempt to grapple with broader socioeconomic issues and especially with those afflicting the nation's minority youth.

NEED FOR A NATIONAL PUBLIC POLICY PROCESS

If the United States is to sustain its military and economic stature in an increasingly dangerous and competitive international milieu, it is imperative that the need for a more effective public process, capable of making appropriate national educational policy, be recognized and acted on. Continued failure to develop an appropriate national structure will guarantee the perpetuation of a nation at risk.

The persistence of a parochial educational policy process in an era of fundamentally national and international concerns raises serious question as to whether it will be possible for the United States to ensure, for posterity, desired levels of civility, socialization, and technological development—or democratic involvement and participation requisite to our persistence as a free and prosperous nation. A system of education where the most essential and fundamental decisions regarding our country's youth (e.g., what every American youth should know and be able to do; how and to what standards this knowledge and these values should be made available; by whom; in what fashion; at what and at whose expense) are made in relative isolation by thousands of quasi-independent school boards and teacher unions may not be adequate to sustain this nation in the twenty-first century. If this argument has substance, the nation may truly be at risk. And if so, the plethora of commission reports and recommendations, to the extent they ignore this vital issue, will contribute little to our collective capacity to confront this crisis. If this hypothesis is valid, to what can we attribute the failure of the many studies to advance boldly fundamental structural and governance reforms? Surely the absence of an effective public process to conceive, formulate, and implement authoritative national educational policy is in part responsible for this dilemma. The resultant policy vacuum contributes to episodic, unpredictable, and at times self-serving policy-making by professors, politicians, preachers, governors, foundations, and associations. This informal, essentially private national policy process is discussed in Chapter 3.

It is important to note at the very outset of this study that what is *not* required, or proposed, is the substitution of a highly centralized system of educational governance and policy-making for the existing parochial process. What is needed first is an awareness of the limitations of the current policy process and its corollary obsession with a narrowly conceived view of school and schooling as the essential base for relevant reform. This concern is described and analyzed at considerable length in Chapter 4.

A second requirement involves suggesting alternative governance and policy processes capable of sustaining and even strengthening the participation of educational professionals, parents, and local citizenry while at the same time providing for an authoritative policy role for the nation's government. A number of such alternatives are presented in the following chapters.

A PRIVATE NATIONAL EDUCATIONAL POLICY PROCESS

To advance the proposition that the nation does not possess a public structure for making fundamental national educational policy, however, is not to suggest that important policy is not developed, debated, and advanced. Certainly the plethora of studies, reports, and proposals for reform, summarized above, vividly argue the contrary. But in contrast to the structure that characterizes national educational policy-making nearly everywhere else in the developed world, the process in the United States, for the reasons alluded to, is peculiarly informal, private, diffuse, episodic, and from a public policy point of view, unaccountable.

Over the past half century the United States, in the absence of a formal process for making fundamental national educational policy, has evolved a nonpublic, essentially private system. This private policy structure, in the absence of a public process, provided the nation with a minimal capability for national educational policy and governance. In subsequent chapters it is argued that the cast of institutions and actors is relatively finite and identifiable. Included are the obvious professional associations and their key leaders, the U.S. Department of Education (USDE) personnel as well as a few members of Congress and their staffs; also important are a handful of private nonprofit foundations and educational institutions. Included in this intricate network are key faculty and administrators from a small number of the nation's leading universities, as well as a few respected educational journalists. Also important are a number of education "umbrella organizations," union leaders, and textbook publishers.

As long as the function of education in the United States was essentially to equip an emergent generation with the knowledge, skills, and values requisite to an adult life not significantly different, or far removed, from that of the local community, the absence of a structured public policy process at the national level did not act to place the nation at risk. However, the United States, about to venture on to the troubled seas of the twenty-first century, is a very different nation from the country our forefathers knew. The challenges the nation faces today are radically different from the challenges for which the current system of education was designed and that, for more than a century, it served well. Twenty-first-century America is, at the same time, more homogeneous and heterogeneous. Over the past half century, the nation has moved to global center stage in an increasingly tumultuous, factional, and interdependent universe. As the United States approaches the complexities of the twenty-first century, the price that it pays for the absence of an effective and relevant public process for evolving and implementing national educational policy is problematically high.

In nearly all developed nations, critical decisions as to what should be taught to whom, for what purpose, by whom, and at whose cost are the product of a public policy process that is an integral part of the functioning of that nation's governmental and political institutions. During the 1960s some American spokespeople, in and out of government, believed that if the United States was to confront the vicissitudes of the twenty-first century successfully, it would be necessary to radically restructure its educational policy process and particularly the respective roles of the various levels of government. Chapter 2 selectively examines attempts to alter significantly the educational policy process during the Kennedy, Johnson, and Carter administrations.

NOTES

1. The National Commission on Excellence in Education, *A Nation at Risk: The Imperative for Educational Reform* (Washington, D.C.: Government Printing Office, 1983), 5.

2. In 1985 Terrel Bell resigned from the Reagan administration and returned to the University of Utah faculty.

3. Mortimer J. Adler, *The Paideia Proposal* (New York: Macmillan, 1982); Task Force on Education for Economic Growth, *Action for Excellence* (Denver: Education Commission of the States, 1983); John Goodlad, *A Place Called School: Prospects for the Future* (New York: McGraw-Hill, 1983); Ernest L. Boyer, *High School: A Report on Secondary Education in America* (New York: Harper and Row, Inc., 1983); Twentieth Century Fund Task Force on Federal Elementary and Secondary Education Policy, *Making the Grade* (1983); Theodore R. Sizer, *Horace's Compromise: The Dilemma of the American High School* (Boston: Houghton-Mifflin Co., 1984); Carnegie Forum on Education and the Economy, *A Nation Prepared: Teachers for the 21st Century* (Hyattsville, 1986); Institute for Educational Leadership, *School Boards: Strengthening Grass Roots Leadership* (Washington, D.C.: Institute for Educational Leadership, 1986); Research and Policy Committee of the Committee for Economic Development, *Children in Need: Investment Strategies for the Educationally Disadvantaged* (New York: Committee for Economic Development, 1987); Youth and America's Future, *The Forgotten Half: Non-College Youth in America* (Washington, D.C.: William T. Grant Foundation Commission on Work, Family and Citizenship, 1988); Ernest L. Boyer, *An Imperiled Generation: Saving Urban Schools* (Princeton: Carnegie Foundation for the Advancement of Teaching, 1988); Commission on Minority Participation in Education and American Life, *One-Third of a Nation* (Washington, D.C.: American Council on Education and Education Commission of the States, 1988); Children's Defense Fund, *A Call for Action to Make Our Nation Safe for Children* (Washington, D.C.: Children's Defense Fund, 1988); Carnegie Council on Adolescent Development, *Turning Points: Preparing Youth for the 21st Century* (New York: Carnegie Corporation of New York, 1989).

4. The 1987 report of the Committee for Economic Development, *Children in Need*, is a welcome departure from the essential uniformity of most of the studies.

5. Graham Down, "Assassins of Excellence," in *The Great School Debate: Which Way for American Education?*, ed. Beatrice Gross and Ronald Gross (New York: Simon and Schuster, 1985), 273. Down particularly noted the failure to focus on the extraordinary inequality of resource allocation for poor and minority children and youth.

6. *A Call for Action to Make Our Nation Safe for Children; An Imperiled Generation; The Forgotten Half; Turning Points.*

2

Federal Role in Perspective

SOME HISTORICAL ANTECEDENTS

In the absence of a clearly defined role the federal government's concern and involvement in public education has historically been ambivalent and cautious. The fact that the American colonies were settled in part to enable religious minorities to find a refuge and a homeland congenial to freedom of worship contributed to the evolution of a peculiarly parochial attitude toward educational policy-making. The primary responsibility of the eighteenth-century schools in most of the American colonies was to provide religious training and a level of basic skills instruction adequate to read the approved version of the Bible and related theological tracts. Not surprisingly, these frontier theocracies viewed with suspicion any suggestion that educational policy either be separated from the founding church or, worse still, be removed to a distant, and possibly theologically unsympathetic, central jurisdiction. For it was just this kind of threat and the fear of persecution that led many of the colonists to brave the North American wilds.

The Founding Fathers who gathered in Philadelphia 200 years

ago to attempt to create a nation from a coterie of fiercely independent near theocracies were themselves products of this heritage. Thus, there was little reason to argue about where jurisdiction for education should properly rest. It was generally assumed that it would remain the responsibility of the local/parish community and that its theological supportive mission would continue. However, this is not to suggest that the Founding Fathers were somehow immune to controversy concerning the intergovernmental allocation of powers, a subject critically important to contemporary educational reform. For, indeed, debate as to the authority and responsibilities of the various levels of government was a constant, and not always harmonious, item on their agenda.

> [T]he perennial debate did not cease with independence: for the allocation of power, by whom, for how long, over whom, and for what social good, occupied the energies and intelligence of our constitutional forefathers, in Philadelphia far into the night, and indeed, drove some to seek the momentary sanity of Philadelphia's neighborhood taverns—it has always been thus in Philadelphia.[1]

It is important that we take note of this historical dimension, for it does much to explain the passion with which Americans have proclaimed and defended the concept of local control of education. The possibility of shifting public service responsibilities, other than education, from local to state jurisdiction, or even to the jurisdiction of the federal government, has never generated comparable controversy.

The federal nature of the constitution and particularly the reserve clause of the Tenth Amendment firmly anchored these traditional values into the fundamental law and custom of the land. Subsequent interpretations of the Constitution, as we shall have occasion to note, have both added to and detracted from the basic principle of local control of public education. Unlike subsequent Supreme Court interpretations and the more recent views of former attorney general Edwin Meese upholding the doctrine of original intent, some of the Founding Fathers were less sure of their infallibility. James Madison, for example, anticipated a dynamic nation and therefore was not of the view that the Constitution was chiseled in stone. He believed that of necessity it would stretch and bend with the changing manner in which "We the people" perceived our problems and needs and how indeed we might best then structure our institutions to secure the commonweal. In *Federalist 46* Madison mused that in some distant future the descendants of these same new Americans might become "more partial to Federal than state government." He predicted that if this pragmatic breed of men were to come to believe that "better administration" were to flow from Washington than from Boston, the nation would inevitably accommodate itself to this new reality. He said that if this were to occur, "the people ought not surely to be precluded from giving most of their confidence where they may discover it to be most due."[2]

In times of national peril and in a few isolated cases where influential spokespeople argued for an expanded role for the federal government, sporadic attempts to modify significantly the governance of public education have occurred. A brief review of some of these efforts is presented to illustrate the relative powerlessness of the federal government to develop a significant educational policy capability in the face of a tenacious tradition of local control, constitutional prescription, and judicial interpretation.

EARLY EFFORTS TO CENTRALIZE EDUCATIONAL GOVERNANCE

During the nineteenth century, controversy concerning the governance of education centered on the issue of school district consolidation and state-imposed uniform regulations; both were opposed by local authorities. The sensitivity of nineteenth-century advocates of local control to what they perceived as fundamentally improper, if not illegal, state initiatives is similar to contemporary concerns over the possibility of an expanded federal role in the governance of education. The following is not the contemporary position of the National School Boards Association but of an 1840 vintage Massachusetts state legislature reacting to Horace Mann's proposal to establish a state board of education: "The establishment of a Board of Education seems to be the commencement of a system of centralization and of monopoly power in a few hands, contrary in every respect, to the true spirit of our democratical institutions."[3] This writer can assure the reader that this point of view persists. As commissioner of education in two states over a period of twelve years, I was often taken to task by hostile school board members and reminded that local control was "a constitutional right" or that state regulation was "contrary to the law of the land"; and on occasion, some of the more passionate advocates went so far as to suggest that violations of local control were contrary to the laws of the Almighty.

The gradual evolution of state regulatory authority over local districts was accompanied by considerable and protracted controversy. However, it was usually—but not always—accompanied by a grudging recognition that state government was at least legally a legitimate, if not a desirable, partner in the provision of public education. But this reluctant acceptance of the state as a bona fide partner was not extended to the federal government. In many of the original thirteen colonies a subsequent state role in education was legitimized by religious homogeneity and tradition. A federal government, a dangerous experiment at best, was blessed with neither long tradition nor religious homogeneity and therefore was not about to be considered seriously as a partner as far as educational policy-making was concerned. The difference between a perceived threat to local control from the actions of the state, on the one hand, and from the actions of the federal government, on the other, is important, for it is not simply a question of degree; it is rather a difference in kind.

Federal involvement in education in the nineteenth and twentieth century was rare and not of great import. Thomas Jefferson was one of the few Founding Fathers who contended that education was critical not solely because it affected the interests of church, community, and even state, but also because the new nation's destiny was a factor that needed to be taken into consideration. He argued that a democratic government depended on a literate and educated citizenry. Jefferson's advocacy of a comprehensive system of education for preindependence Virginia anticipated the advent of the "common school" and an expanded state involvement that were to occur a century later. However, with the exception of a proposal for a National University advanced by George Washington, Jefferson, Benjamin Rush, and others, there is little evidence suggesting that the Founding Fathers anticipated a significant or direct federal role in the education of the nation's children and youth.

Even a brief discussion of the role of the federal government in public education during this era must note the Land Ordinances of 1785 and 1787. Certainly the requirement that a portion of the western territories be reserved to support public schools suggests that even in the Republic's infancy federal lawmakers, at least under certain circumstances, were prepared to dedicate federal resources for educational purposes. The language of the Land Ordinance of 1787 explicitly justifies federal support for public education as a means of securing "good government."

The Morrill Act (1862), which dedicated proceeds from the sale of federal lands to the states to establish colleges of agriculture and engineering, is an early indication of the relative willingness of the federal government to be relatively more proactive in public higher education than in matters related to the public schools. The relative absence of jurisdictional disputes over the governance of public higher education is partly attributable to the fact that the land grant universities, in contrast to public schools, were established after, and not prior to, independence. Opposition to a significant federal role in public higher education traditionally is more likely to come from the private colleges and universities than from state or local governments.

The U.S. Office of Education was established in 1867. At its very inception its role was narrowly circumscribed, limited essentially to the gathering of statistics and later to research on teaching methods, and so on—hardly an incipient Ministry of Education.

Never quite sure as to just what role it should play, Congress, on occasion, has assigned it a variety of seemingly unrelated tasks including a demographic study of Alaska's moose!

The passage of the 1913 Income Tax Amendment, which ushered in an era of revenue transfer from Washington to the state and local governments, was prerequisite to an expanded educational role for the federal government. The Smith-Hughes Act (1917), which provided federal funds for vocational education, at first glance appears contrary to the traditional reluctance of the federal government to become proactively involved in public elementary and secondary education.[4] However, it is important to recall that the national interest was involved: The war effort was dependent on a supply of skilled manpower. As we shall have occasions to note, perceived threats to national security by foreign powers act to dilute local control and legitimize an expanded federal role in education.

By granting funds to the states for an explicit educational purpose with a minimum of direct federal involvement, the Smith-Hughes Act established an important precedent—one that essentially provided the model for nearly all subsequent programs. The legislation required matching state dollars and the submittal of an acceptable "state plan." This then-novel requirement—that funding was dependent on meeting federal conditions and abiding by federal regulations—anticipated a policy process that became increasingly common after 1960. The Smith-Hughes precedent, which made the availability of federal funds contingent on their being targeted for limited purposes and for specific children, enabled the federal government to exercise some influence on overall educational policy, without the necessity of attempting to secure fundamental changes in law and custom. But a price was paid: From this point on, federal educational policy was perceived as supplemental, categorical, child specific, and most important, nonauthoritative. Thus, the Smith-Hughes Act marks an important point in the shaping of a federal role in educational policy-making, for it established the guiding precedent that federal influence would be obtained by the granting or withholding of federal dollars, rather than explicitly through legislative authority. It also had the effect of establishing the basis for a unique interdependence of state and federal bureaucracies.

Over time state and local interest groups evolved to exert pressure on Congress to provide desirable levels of funding and on the federal bureaucracy to minimize regulation. Congress and the administration, in turn, effectively negotiated federal dollars for policies and programs carried out by state and local educational agencies that were perceived to be in the national interest. As in most political accommodations that survive, both parties secured some, but not all, of their interests. While fundamental educational policy-making remained at the state and local levels, the federal government gradually came to accept the precept that the national interest in education was not something to be conceived broadly and legislated but rather something to be negotiated with fifty state agencies and, of course indirectly, with some 16,000 school districts.

The Great Depression and the New Deal, which it spawned, significantly shaped the evolving American federalism, which in turn set the stage for the efforts of the 1960s to forge a significant proactive educational role for the national government. The preoccupation of the early Roosevelt era with domestic problems and related legislation did not, as one might have expected, lead to a significant change in educational governance or policy-making. In the United States the failure of the schools to deliver youth employment traditionally has the effect of questioning the system's validity but does not lead to profound reform. In England as well as in other Western democracies, on the other hand, youth unemployment has led to significant changes in the governance of public education—usually in the direction of enhanced central control. In the United States, however, the federal system and a long tradition of local control acted to divert federal legislation and programs directly addressing the "depression" problems of children and youth away from the nation's parochial system of public education. Initiatives such as the Civilian Conservation Corps and the National Youth Administration were deliberately distanced from the public school system and instead were channeled through the Departments of Labor, Interior, and Agriculture. Avoiding the federal education agencies served to circumvent the forces of local control and states' rights.

During the New Deal era the federal government, bypassing the states, increasingly made funds directly available to local governments but almost never to local educational authorities. This practice of using federal funds to lever local resources to address a perceived national interest was not extended to local school districts. The effect of excluding local school districts from New Deal grants made directly to localities, in conjunction with a deliberate strategy of funding youth programs outside state and local educational channels, was to distance further the federal government from a direct role in educational policy-making. As we have occasion to note below, the precedents established during this era no doubt influenced the design and formulation of youth policy in the 1960s and 1970s and will likely help shape policy for the 1990s and beyond.

POSTWAR EFFORTS TO EXPAND
THE FEDERAL ROLE

The first—and to date, the last—significant direct transfer of general-purpose federal dollars to local school districts occurred during World War II and then again during the Korean War in an effort to compensate localities for the additional expenses encumbered in providing educational services for children housed on, or in proximity to, military facilities. This precedent of providing general aid directly to local school districts did not go unnoticed by those who had long sought to elicit noncategorical federal support for education. The NEA was quick to see the possible precedent and lobbied persistently for legislation that would provide substantial federal funding directly to local school districts that would be neither child nor program specific.

The battle to secure significant "general aid" from the federal government intensified during the 1950s as hard-pressed school systems sought to accommodate the burgeoning educational demands unleashed by the postwar baby boom. Legislation to provide general aid was introduced on a number of occasions and as early as 1948. However, the efforts of the NEA and other interested associations to carve out a major role for the federal government in educational funding, if not policy, was strongly and successfully resisted by the combined opposition of the many diverse proponents of local control. The National School Boards Association and other champions of local control feared that the provision of substantial general federal funding for school construction and teacher salaries would allow the camel's nose to penetrate the educational tent dangerously.The policy of general direct educational aid was also resisted by the opponents of school desegregation, who feared that an enhanced proactive federal role would jeopardize segregated schools. It was also opposed by the proponents of church-related education who were concerned that their competitive position vis-à-vis the public schools would be adversely affected.

It is interesting to speculate as to what the educational policy role of the federal government might have been had the efforts to secure general federal support of schools succeeded. It is conceivable that gradually increasing federal support, accompanied by a decline in local and possibly state support, would have heralded, for better or for worse, a truly national system of public education.

Sputnik and the resulting fear that the nation was in danger of losing its preeminence in science and technology to its Soviet competitors led many to conclude that Soviet schools were superior to American. The consequent passage of the National Defense Education Act (NDEA) (1958), providing for substantial federal support for science, math, and foreign language instruction, demonstrated once again the close association between perceived national peril and an inclination toward a relatively proactive national educational policy. It is doubtful whether the average American is as fearful of the consequences of a greater federal presence in public education as are educators and the educational establishment. "By the end of the 1950s both the Roper and the

Gallup polls showed an increase from two-thirds to three-quarters of Americans favoring outright federal assistance."[5]

Despite the advocacy of powerful interest groups and public opinion, "general support" legislation languished and the NDEA, the only significant education legislation passed during the 1950s, retained the categorical precedents set out in Smith-Hughes.

The Supreme Court's landmark desegregation decision in *Brown* v. *Topeka Board of Education* (1954), although not intended to expand the federal role in education, may have contributed more to the spate of significant federal educational initiatives of the 1960s and 1970s than the sum of all preceding legislation. This landmark decision not only resulted in relevant legislation and the involvement of the federal government in school desegregation policies and activities but also led to a growing awareness of the national implications and consequences of severe educational inequality. Nonetheless, the powerful values and policy precedents that historically limited a significant educational role for the federal government to times of national peril, and then to limited, categorically defined targets, persisted during the tumultuous 1960s and 1970s. The reasons are powerful and consistent, as Hugh Davis Graham notes:

> For to propose federal intrusion into the sanctity of the state-local-private preserve of education was to stride boldly into a uniquely dangerous mine field that pitted Democrat against Republican, liberal against conservative, Catholic against Protestant and Jew, federal power against state's rights, white against black, and rich constituency against poor in mercurial cross-cutting alliances.[6]

THE KENNEDY AND JOHNSON YEARS

The 1960 Nixon–Kennedy campaign launched a new era in the politics of American education. It was the first to raise education as a major partisan issue. Neither Nixon nor Kennedy found it politically prudent to advocate categorically an enhanced federal role in education. In his campaign speeches John Kennedy, however, did frequently pledge his administration to federal funding to help raise teacher salaries and assist in school construction. Implicit in these campaign promises was at least the possibility of general aid. But political rhetoric advocating new federal dollars for public education was nearly always accompanied by a disclaimer with respect to any implied intentions of altering the governance status quo or in any way diminishing states' rights or local control.

Prior to his inauguration Kennedy established a number of transition task forces, including one on education headed by Frederick Hovde, president of Purdue University. Key members of this task force—persons who would subsequently play important roles in shaping the educational policies of the Kennedy and Johnson years—included John Gardner, president of the Carnegie Foundation; Francis Keppel, dean of the Harvard Graduate School of Education; and Alvin Eurich, a Ford Foundation vice president.

The task force report, prematurely released, called for a radically expanded role for the federal government to the tune of a whopping $9.25 billion to be expended over a four-and-one-half-year period. Adding to the controversial magnitude of the proposed program was the recommendation that about two-thirds of this sum be reserved exclusively for institutions of public education, a point not overlooked by the Catholic hierarchy. The recommended formula for distributing this surprising largess left little doubt but that the task force was recommending a fundamental departure from the traditional role of ad hoc limited-purpose categorical assistance. For example, it was proposed that a general per pupil grant be made available to local school districts, according to a formula that would significantly compensate for poverty conditions.[7] The audacity and boldness of these proposals were only exceeded by their political naïveté; there was little likelihood that a program of this extraordinary magnitude, that had managed to antagonize the private school sector and that gave the defenders of local control reason to believe that the fiery tongue of the federal dragon was about to descend on them, would ever see the light of day.

Despite efforts to meet the multiple objections of various impacted constituencies, Kennedy's 1961 education package failed to receive congressional approval. A subsequent effort the following year while retaining the philosophy of direct general per pupil aid considerably scaled down the dollars involved. However, it met with a similar unhappy fate.

The president was faced not only with the opposition of the Catholic hierarchy, southern conservatives, and local control advocates but by many in his own administration who did not highly regard the capability or the impartiality of the state and local educational administrators who would be required to manage and expend these substantial general-purpose monies. Few of the key persons charged by the Kennedy administration with responsibility for developing and shepherding the legislative package had had any experience in either state or local educational institutions and tended to regard this vast bureaucratic army with considerable suspicion and disdain. Indeed, many were convinced that a combination of local and state ineptness and even venality would simply guarantee that a massive federal general aid program, devoid of the regulatory detail that accompanied categorical grants, would but fail massively. The new era architects

> knew, if not empirically then intuitively, that it was the SEAs (State Education Agencies) that had lo these many years posed the major obstacle to our realizing the final mile of the long journey towards equality and plenty. The SEA was regarded as a bastion of rural interests, staffed by teacher college produced bureaucrats, in league with equally incompetent school administrators, employing their traditional monopoly over the allocation of educational resources to maintain a self interested status-quo and thereby their own sinecures, all at the expense of continued injustice, perpetual ignorance, and a class determined poverty.[8]

President Kennedy's new frontiersmen barely had time to organize their touch football leagues before the racial animosities smoldering in the nation's ghettos began to erupt. The alienation and anger that in the early 1960s exploded, city after city, into violence came as a surprise to most observers of the nation's social scene. The Ford Foundation and especially Paul Ylvisaker were among the first to appreciate the growing nexus connecting postwar urban poverty, minority youth alienation, and violence. Ylvisaker made the pilgrimage to Washington, where he joined the ranks of the new frontier, and consistent with a pattern discussed at some length below, he completed the cycle at Harvard's Graduate School of Education. Along with such colleagues as Harold Howe and Francis Keppel, whose career migrations were similar, he has exercised considerable influence on the nation's youth and educational policies.

As the dimensions and severity of the minority/urban/poverty problems became increasingly apparent, the Kennedy administration bureaucrats, drawing heavily on their academic contacts, formulated a host of programmatic responses. Academicians, few of whom had ever seen, let alone experienced, the plight of poor urban youth, were summoned to Washington to render their often conflicting and sometimes naive diagnoses and remedies. The school of thought advocating "Community Action," although strongly opposed by those favoring more traditional bureaucratic approaches, won the day. Community Action was difficult to oppose. After all, it was democratic and procommunity and involved the participation and wishes of the poor urban residents. In operation the concept was imprecisely defined and more of an ideology than an operating principle. It generally required that the federal agency involved, more often the Office of Economic Opportunity, identify sympathetic, and preferably affected, locals who would be cajoled into organizing a planning/management council that would employ the federal funds to remedy their perceived problems. Nearly anything went, so long as it emphasized community involvement and prohibited any heavy-handed direction from existing governmental institutions.

The naïveté of the nation's academic/intellectual elite concerning the efficacy and probable propriety of the often romanticized Community Action organizations is a persistent and powerful theme in the history of American social thought and action. And as we have a number of occasions to note, this theme persists as a major factor influencing contemporary policy initiatives and reform proposals.

The seductive allure of the parochial, ad hoc Community Action process has long acted to confuse ends and means. There is little evidence to support the fact that this myriad of programs did much to address its targeted problems, whereas there are considerable data indicating that the funds were often misspent and unaccounted for.

In an excellent analysis of the policies of the War on Poverty Nicholas Lemann concludes:

> Community action . . . was based on the idea that only through local efforts . . . inside the poorest neighborhoods, could the Government increase opportunity. How, it now seems fair to ask, could there have been so much faith in the ability of a program inside the ghettoes to increase the opportunities available to the people living there?[9]

President Lyndon Johnson was less sanguine than either of the Kennedys that the Community Action approach was an effective weapon in the War on Poverty, possibly because he had firsthand experience of local poverty and related institutional responses. Sargent Shriver, President Johnson's point man in the poverty war, advanced a variety of approaches to the worsening dilemma of urban youth alienation and violence. One of these, the Job Corps, about which we have more to say in Chapter 7, embraced an essentially opposite philosophy from that of Community Action. Whereas Community Action looked to local people to solve their problems within the community, the Job Corps acted to move the alienated youth out of the ghetto to distant residential camps where training and educational programs were designed and run by government agencies or by corporate contractors.

Many of the enthusiastic young men that labored mightily to design and implement this bold new educational policy had been recruited from the ranks of university scholars and administrators. It is important to draw attention to the tendency to recruit the new education era architects from academe and especially from such prestigious institutions as Harvard, Columbia, and Berkeley, for they brought with them a related perspective on governance that did much to shape resultant policy proposals.

More than a quarter century of observation from the vantage point of both academia and government has convinced me that university scholars are peculiarly inclined to view institutional authority, and especially government, with studied suspicion and disdain. I suspect that many of my esteemed colleagues were drawn to academic careers, despite the relative paucity of material rewards, because for one reason or another they were born anarchists! A university environment not only provides a unique haven for a would-be anarchist but frosts the cake by permitting him or her the extraordinary pleasure of slaying, with near impunity, authoritarian dragons. As one who has been both slayer and slayee, I have also noted that the scholar's suspicion and distrust of bureaucratic and political realms are in direct proportion to the relative level of the polity at issue. The most feared and thus most inclined to be denied a place at the table are the dragons in Washington—unless and when one is himself or herself, at least temporarily, occupying one of those seats of power. Being somewhat closer to anarchical verities, state politicians and bureaucrats are less feared if not less respected. The closer one moves to a Rousseauistic state of natural anarchy, the less threatening and more relatively acceptable becomes any political institution. Academic writers and scholars in the field of education, with very few exceptions, consistently argue in favor of maximizing the authority of the classroom teacher and of limiting that of ascending levels of the hierarchy. Thus, the authority of the school building is to be preferred over that of the district, and that of the district over the state, and if it comes to that, the state over the federal government. Some carry the logic to the point of advocating that fundamental decisions about education should be left to the family.[10]

Respected scholars such as Arthur Wise warn us of the creeping growth of the public sector in our lives, a growth that is particularly apparent at the stage and national levels.[11] Underlying this philosophy is a firm belief that "that government which governs least governs best." Ironically it is often these same scholars who while advocating a narrow limitation on the role of government simultaneously champion the rights of the disadvantaged and dispossessed—functionally liberal and structurally conservative.

A major force propelling the trend toward more centralized educational policy-making is the response to the long-neglected needs of minorities: racial, ethnic, economic, handicapped, and so on. Appeal to a more inclusive level of authority by minorities who believe that their rights and interests are being denied has long been an integral attribute of the American political system. Wise and others argue that this process of appeal to a more inclusive political institution erodes local control and foments centralization. Perhaps. But it also safeguards individual and minority rights from capricious community action. Women who appeal a denial of their individual rights, parents who appeal the treatment of their handicapped child, and an ethnic association that appeals the denial of services for non-English-speaking children may in the process be eroding local control and promoting centralization. However, it is important that we not lose sight of the fact that the fundamental issues at stake are not ones of governance but rather ones of the educational rights and needs of children.

In late 1962, still determined to obtain educational legislation, the Kennedy administration, increasingly aware of where the land mines were located, sought to defuse some of the controversial issues by wrapping educational reform in a larger social welfare package. The persistence of the traditional opposition to an enhanced federal role in education led the Kennedy administration, as it did its successors, to attempt to achieve its policy objectives by circumventing the parochial educational swamp and moving its legislative package via alternative channels. The 1962 omnibus bill, for example, cloaked educational reforms in a social welfare wrapping. Such a strategy, it was believed, could effectively neutralize the traditional opposition to a proactive federal presence and at the same time build alternative supporting coalitions. A strategy of circumventing the educational establishment and its parochial governance structures, as we shall have occasions to note, was also resorted to by the Johnson administration—but with considerably greater success. The 1963 omnibus bill strategically emphasized less "education" than it did the needs of the nation's "youth." It included, for example, provisions for manpower training and for a domestic-type Peace Corps.[12] However, provisions in the bill that would have augmented public school teacher salaries and provided general aid to assist in school construction doomed the proposed legislation to a fate identical to that of its hapless predecessor. More successful attempts at reform would have to await the advent of Johnson's political savvy.

As one of his last major personnel decisions President Kennedy appointed Dean Francis Keppel of Harvard University's Graduate School of Education to fill the vacant position of commissioner of education in the Department of Health, Education, and Welfare. Back at Harvard after a distinguished career in government, Keppel continues to play an important and influential role.

THE GREAT SOCIETY AND THE FEDERAL ROLE

In 1964 the Johnson administration, having studied the failed efforts of its predecessor, took much of the substance of the Kennedy educational agenda and incorporated it into its comprehensive antipoverty legislative package. As with the Kennedy administration, the Johnson team turned for policy ideas and strategies to a number of task forces composed primarily of government and university representatives. The important task force on education was chaired by John Garner, president of the Carnegie Foundation. Subsequently, President Johnson asked Gardner to chair the 1965 White House Conference on Education and in the same year appointed him secretary of Health, Education, and Welfare (HEW). Commissioner Keppel, a close friend of Gardner's, played a key role on the task force. Keppel's father, like Gardner, had once served as president of the Carnegie Foundation.[13] Keppel was instrumental in the recruitment of the task force members. When Keppel sought a new deputy for the Office of Education, he turned to Henry Loomis, a former Harvard colleague and also a friend of Gardner's. In 1965, having run afoul of the political wrath of Mayor Richard Daley, Keppel was "promoted" to a new position as assistant secretary of HEW for Education. He was replaced as commissioner of education by Harold Howe III, who held the position until 1968. Howe is currently Senior Lecturer at Harvard University's Graduate School of Education and among the most influential spokespeople on matters concerning youth and educational policy.

The work of the task force culminated in the language that emerged as the Elementary and Secondary Education Act of 1964, the most sweeping and significant federal educational legislation in the nation's history. The success of the Johnson package is in part attributable to the fact that it abandoned efforts to obtain general aid and returned to seeking funding for carefully targeted categorical programs. This strategy of packaging the reforms in a number of separate titles, each with its own distinctive purpose and client target, also had the effect of creating parallel interest groups that effectively promoted the concerns and funding levels of their respective programs. The numerous well-funded interest groups that evolved in response to the categorical components of the Great Society's education agenda naturally developed a vested interest in the maintenance and perpetuation of the many programs targeted to special clients. Thus, a tenacious defense of the interests of the respective special populations effectively argued against an alternative strategy of general aid. The narrow categorical approach was also supported by federal bureaucrats who had little confidence in the ability of the state and local authorities to handle increased responsibility "properly." By packaging the legislation in circumscribed categorical programs, each with its accompanying array of detailed regulation, it was thought possible to ensure rigorous federal bureaucratic oversight.

The Johnson years witnessed a major breakthrough in the provision of substantial federal dollars for education. However, the price paid for this relative largess was the persistence of the traditional safeguards against the evolution of a fundamental proactive policy role for the federal government in American education. Despite growing evidence that such a role was necessary, the forces of localism, federalism, and religion, abetted by categorically oriented bureaucracies and interest groups at the various levels of governance, prevailed in their determination to maintain the status quo.

The Nixon and Ford administrations sought with little success to cut back on support for the programs launched during the Johnson years but, with one exception noted below, did not attempt to seek fundamental changes in the role of the federal government. The Nixon administration's efforts to substitute revenue sharing for categorical programs might be viewed as a movement in the direction of general aid and thereby toward a potentially enlarged role for the federal government. However, it is quite apparent that the motivation of the Nixon administration was less one of enhancing the federal government's influence than it was of cutting expenditures and shrinking the role of government generally.

THE ESTABLISHMENT OF
THE DEPARTMENT OF EDUCATION

The Carter administration's concern with public education was dominated by its efforts to establish the Department of Education. As with his predecessors, president-elect Carter dutifully established the expected transition committees, which just as dutifully prepared an avalanche of recommendations, most of which were read by few others than their authors. Obviously, this writer's views concerning the necessity of perceiving education in a broad, relatively holistic manner have not changed much since 1975 when he prepared the following remarks for the Carter education transition team:

> When suggesting educational priorities for a new administration one must guard against the professional temptation to view educational policy in isolation from its social context. Educational policy only makes sense if it relates to more fundamental goals or issues. Education is the foundation for developing and directing fundamental social policy. Accordingly, educational priorities must be shaped to address the issues and problems confronting our society.[14]

The concerns expressed throughout this book that the existing parochial governance structure is incapable of coping with the increasingly national dimensions of the youth and education crisis were already formulated some fifteen years ago: "Although the governance of public education is essentially and constitutionally a state responsibility shared with thousands of local school districts, federal policy cannot be blind to the increasing failure of the traditional governance mechanisms in public education to cope with the major elements" afflicting American youth.[15]

THE FEDERAL ROLE IN THE REAGAN YEARS

The rhetoric of the 1980 campaign and the immediate postelection skirmishes seemed to preview a radical retrenchment of the federal role in education. The new administration heralded a Reagan revolution, promising a restoration of the nation's tarnished international respect and prowess; a reassertion of the dignity and rights of individual Americans, which, it was argued, had fallen prey to increasingly impersonal and remote bureaucracies; and a reassertion of the traditional American virtues of family, church, and work ethic. As for bread and butter domestic issues, the stuff of which the new society was formed, in the Reagan era were perceived as the cause rather than as the resolution of the nation's malaise. The problems of American education, in the eyes of the Reaganites, were not those of too little federal involvement and too few federal dollars but of too much of both. This conclusion obviously suggested its own strategy: cut expenditures for education. Indeed, some of the more stalwart conservatives argued that all federal dollars for education should be terminated. A major Reagan appointee in the Office of Policy Development stated that "block grants [as opposed to the inherited policy of categorical grants] are the first step toward total withdrawal of the federal government from education."[16] The federal role, it was argued, should at least be returned to the intent of the Founding Fathers. Thus, the ill-begotten Department of Education must go! And if anything were to remain in its stead, it should be limited to the intended role of the Office of Education: the collection of statistics.

Shortly after his inauguration President Ronald Reagan, in a major televised address, informed the American people that he was proposing a major restructuring of the federal government's role in education. Specifically he informed his fellow citizens that he intended to unravel a near half century of creeping educational socialism promulgated under the guise of the New Deal and the Great Society. His plans called for a massive reduction in federal expenditures for education, combining those categorical programs that could not immediately be discontinued into preferably one, but at the least into a very few block grants to the states. Ideally the result of these policies would be a massive reversal in the long trend toward increased federal involvement in public education and a return of this basic public service to state and local jurisdictions and, where possible, to the family, where the Founding Fathers, the people, and God intended them to be. In an address to the National School Boards Association, Dennis Doyle, then director of Educational Policy Studies at the American Enterprise Institute, laid out the future as envisaged by the administration:

The election of a conservative national government is merely the proximate cause of the transfer of power in education to the states. The election of 1980 only mirrors the changing facts and social forces that fuel and drive the shift. From now on, your schools will be forced to compete with other programs for progressively scarce resources. And as the federal role decreases, your main battlegrounds will be the states.[17]

The coup de grace to the Reagan revolution's educational battle was to be the elimination of the ill-conceived and ill-begotten Department of Education. And indeed legislation to achieve this goal was promptly introduced. Although the administration was initially successful in considerably reducing the level of federal expenditures for education, and did achieve some consolidation, Congress diluted these efforts and was able to frustrate the president's determined attempt to abolish the Department of Education and bring about major program consolidation.

Some of the president's more ardent supporters entreated that he do nothing less than abolish not only the Department of Education but the entire foundation of public education in America. Former Secretary of Education Terrel Bell with both pain and humor quotes one such right wing radical:

Schools are necessary but they can be created by free enterprise today as they were before the public school movement achieved its fraudulent state monopoly in education. . . . The failure of public education is the failure of statism as a political philosophy. . . . The system cannot work because in a free society government has no more place in education than it does in religion.[18]

Possibly the failure of the Reagan administration to scrap the Department of Education is attributable less to the strength of the opposition than to its own ineptness. Reagan's right wing critics were dumbstruck by his appointment of Terrel Bell as secretary. After all, Bell had served in the Carter administration and had himself once testified before Congress in support of the department. Was it ineptness or cunning that led to the Bell appointment? Bell himself is not certain: "I am not sure why I was chosen by the President, especially in view of the fact that I had once testified favorably on the bill that created the Department of Education."[19] There never seemed much doubt as to where this forthright public servant stood on this issue: "My purpose was to preserve the traditional federal role in education. To do so I had to work cautiously with those who wanted to both abolish my department and to scrap nearly the entire federal presence in education."[20]

Whereas the Kennedy and Johnson administrations seemed to be in search of a more proactive role, and an enlarged slice of the governance pie, the Reagan presidency sought to restore education to its traditionally minuscule position in the federal government. Thus, it is not surprising that no explicit plan for education surfaced during these years.

Bell writes that he sought in vain for an explicit administration statement of goals and objectives that could guide policy and strategy.[21] It should have come as no surprise to the secretary that his administration was unable or unwilling to stake out a clear federal role—for indeed there was none. Even the relatively pro-active Kennedy and Johnson administrations carried out a policy of reaction, rather than one of long-range planning based on an explicitly formulated and promulgated federal role.

Unless and until the issue of whether or not the times and circumstances call for a fundamental reexamination of the gover-nance of American education, it is hardly likely that a national policy will emerge. But, as is argued here, unless a capacity and capability to formulate publicly national educational policy emerge in the foreseeable future, there is little likelihood that sustained education reforms commensurate with the nation's ac-knowledged needs will evolve.

The Democrats' successful recapture of Congress in 1986, the unanticipated clarion call of an administration-appointed task force for action at all levels of government to reform American education to rescue a nation at risk, and the preoccupation of the administration with Irangate together all but stifled the Reagan revolution, at least in its plans to revolutionize the educational role of the federal government.

The likelihood that the Reagan revolution, at least in its educational dimensions, had fizzled is suggested by the prominence of educational and related issues in the 1988 presidential campaign. In their respective party primary campaigns all candidates vied to project themselves as *the* education candidate. Senator Albert Gore, for example, advocated that the next president of the United States be remembered as "the education president." Regardless of party, the candidates, including Vice President George Bush, urged more, not fewer, federal dollars for education, and no one except the increasingly isolated right fringe of the Republican party promoted the dismemberment of the Department of Education. The views of the American public sampled in late 1987 revealed a strong desire that education become a major issue in the 1988 election campaigns. Indeed, "education was far out in front, lapping up as much support (31 percent) as health care, arms control, and defense put together."[22] Edward Fiske, the insightful *New York Times* educational writer, succinctly identifies the ambiguity and difficulties faced by our covey of would-be presidents: "No one is quite sure what the Federal role should be in an area that the founding fathers left primarily to state and local governments and where Washington, reluctant to play Santa Claus, still supplies only 8 percent of the money."[23]

The spate of educational reform studies, embraced by the media, captured the attention of a public that discovered even before the politicians and professors that all was not well with the nation's educational enterprise. And there would seem to be little evidence that the public—in contrast to anarchically leaning academic pundits, school board local control enthusiasts, or constitutional strict constructionists—concludes that the federal government's role should inevitably be narrowly proscribed or arbitrarily limited. Despite conclusive evidence that the American public believes that the education of its youth and the welfare of its children constitute a primary concern, both Governor Michael Dukakis and Vice President Bush avoided discussing educational issues in other than general rhetorical terms. The necessity, on the one hand, of addressing the issues of education, child care, and so on, and, on the other hand, of conforming to the strictures of local control and states' rights put the candidates in a dilemma. If they deferred to the hoary traditions of a limited federal role, they were reduced to offering more of the same old remedies that have filled commission and task force reports over the past half century, recommendations that have done little to slow the decline in the quality of American education.

Given the necessity of seeking the lowest political denominator, it is not surprising that the presidential candidates, in the primaries as well as in the general election, tended to latch on to one or a few traditional, essentially noncontroversial remedies and then sought to provide their favorite and safe "twist." None suggested that possibly the governance structure was partially responsible for the persistent failure of the traditional recipes to resolve the educational dilemma. The campaign speeches were replete with good intentions to restore old-fashioned discipline and American values, to raise student and teacher standards, to promote magnet schools and a longer school day or year, to improve literacy programs, to better teacher salaries and working conditions, to provide for merit pay, and to make more testing and evaluation possible. That is not to say, however, that nothing but orthodoxy was preached from the political stump. Pat Robertson, not surprisingly, advocated voluntary prayer in the schools; Governor Dukakis, taking a leaf from the Kennedy campaign, told us that he would seek to establish a volunteer National Teacher Corps; and a number of the right-of-center Republican candidates beat the familiar drum of vouchers and tuition tax credits.

IMPLICATIONS OF A LIMITED FEDERAL ROLE

One factor possibly accounting for the persistent failure of the political dialogue to confront the governance issues afflicting American education, despite a growing recognition that what was required was something more than marginal reform, is the interesting tendency of those occupying the Far Right and Far Left to both come down on the side of little or no federal involvement in public education and to champion the pristine virtues of commu-

nity control and/or family determination. Given the collective
power of this unusual alliance, it is difficult, if not downright
politically risky, for anyone wishing to obtain or retain a career in
politics, academic as well as governmental, to advocate a radical
reallocation of authority and responsibility for the education of the
nation's youth. The power of tradition, buttressed by what the
Constitution does not say, acts to place the remedy of structural
reform outside the limits of allowable debate. A decade ago this
writer, sensing the long-run implications of categorically denying
alterations in the governance structure, wrote that rather than
becoming consumed and preoccupied with what level of government should properly assume responsibility for what aspects of
education, we

> should seek to dispassionately identify at what level, and
> under what conditions, the values we associate with public
> education can best be secured. To do otherwise exposes us to
> the danger that the function of education will come to be
> perceived as the maintenance of a particular decisional struc-
> ture rather than one of maximizing the welfare of the client-
> child. . . . The issue of states' rights [and local control], is
> frequently but a stalking horse employed to perpetuate a
> preferred process of public policy [making], and resource
> allocation—at times tortuously and rhetorically legitimized
> as better for children.[24]

The tenacity of existing structures, which provide many with
power, employment, and patronage, is difficult to gauge, as Governor Mario Cuomo and New York's Mayor Ed Koch recently
discovered. The disarray that characterizes the New York City
school system has triggered a number of proposals by the governor,
the mayor, and others to change the governance structure in a
manner that would essentially lessen the authority of the community school boards while enhancing that of the city board of
education, the mayor, and the state. Predictably, both conservative
politicians and liberal academics attacked the proposed changes—

for different reasons but with the same consequences. Typical are the words of Jane Perlez, writing in the *New York Times* that "most educators express the belief that stressing governance at the expense of change inside the school house is a form of political filibustering."[25] Theodore Sizer, who chaired one of the many studies of "what's wrong with education," remarked that "New York City has a 25 year history of changing the governance chairs and not an awful lot has happened. The politics of the upper echelon have been emphasized rather than the politics of what is needed to help the kids."[26] The reactions of Sizer, currently a distinguished Professor of Education at Brown University (and a product of the Harvard Graduate School of Education), to the proposed changes were predictable, reflecting, as they do, the typical point of view of academicians to proposals that would act to centralize educational governance. Sizer is correct that unfortunately "not a lot has happened" over the past quarter century to improve education in New York City. However, the incidence of change has been far less pronounced in governance than in curriculum reform, teacher training and standards, drop-out prevention programs, bilingual education, countless task forces, and study groups, most dominated by Sizer's colleagues from the world of academe. Surely the failure of decades of pedagogical reform after reform to stay the decline of New York's schools should suggest the possibility that fundamental contributory factors, at least partially, lie elsewhere.

The only significant change in educational governance in New York City over the past half century was the decentralization of authority of education to some thirty-two community school districts. This panacea was in large part concocted and strongly supported by academicians. Few today would argue that this decentralization policy has been a success. Indeed, most now agree that decentralization is partially responsible for the deplorable condition of that city's school system. However, attempts to undo the damage predictably run head on into a powerful defense garbed in the armor of the virtues of local control and community democracy, often a facade for the maintenance of a system that has little to do with the welfare of children and much to do with protecting patronage sources and adult jobs and prerogatives. Ironically, in the face of overwhelming evidence that decentralization of the New York City schools had just the opposite effect of that intended, a number of educators argue that the problem is not enough decentralization. If power to a multitude of what have become highly politicized community school boards is not the solution, then decentralize even further to the building level, give budget authority to the principal, and turn the decisional process over to thousands of parent committees.

In New Jersey, Governor Tom Kean also recently discovered that attempts to expand the authority of the state to permit placing failed school systems in "receivership" elicit the same familiar arguments of the sanctity of local control and of the assumed venality of a distant bureaucracy. With refreshing, though possibly not politically astute, candor Governor Kean, frustrated by his inability, in the face of opposition from the state's school boards, to obtain passage of the necessary legislation, stated, "Some New Jersey school board members do not care about children. . . . The school boards are political. . . . It's got everybody's brother-in-law and campaign manager working for the school boards in some of these situations. . . . They could care less about children."[27] From the vantage point of this writer, who spent some eight years as commission of education in New Jersey, the governor is absolutely correct in his observations.

Fundamental demographic changes that are affecting most of the nation's cities frequently have the effect of pitting the interests of an aging declining white population, striving to maintain control of the political institutions, against those of newly emergent black and Hispanic majorities, whose children make up the greater part of the student body. Governance of many of the nation's decaying cities in effect denies educational opportunity for minority children, who frequently constitute a majority of the school population. School boards in cities that fit this description are not inclined to perceive their role as one of maximizing educational expenditures and services. Clinging tenaciously to its sources of patronage and marching primarily to the drum beat of its support base, the power structure often skews resources in the direction of an aging white clientele. Not surprisingly, the relatively powerless minority community, unimpressed with arguments of local control, turns to the state or to the courts for the legal and political muscle required to ensure that its children receive the educational services to which they are entitled. The state's efforts to respond, as Governor Kean discovered, are sometimes met by accusations that state intervention in the interests of children undermines the very fabric of American society. This pattern of local tyranny disguised as community democracy and local control is not limited to whites over minorities. I have had occasion to deal with similar situations wherein black control of the power structure was employed to limit the educational (and employment) opportunities of a minority Hispanic community.

As the nation accommodates itself to the reality of a new national administration, the issue of how and by whom the country's fundamental education policies should be made remain unresolved. Change has occurred but the essential parameters, whereby the federal government's role is reactive, categorical, and relatively minor, remain fixed. They are summed up well by Secretary Bell, who, though he tenaciously and skillfully sheltered the traditional federal role as it has evolved over the lifetime of the Republic, subscribes to the status quo.

The federal government must play a vital *supportive* role in assisting the states, local communities, and private institutions as they strive to carry out *their* responsibilities in the realm of education. . . . We have assumed a traditional responsibility on the federal level to provide *special* assistance to *help* carry the burden of educating handicapped, minority, and disadvantaged students. We have also assumed federal responsibility for civil rights, enforcement and adherence to the ideals of equal educational opportunity. . . . The federal government can play its role of *supporting and supplementing* the states, localities, and private education agencies, without *intruding* into the delicate areas of control, management and *direction* of the education enterprise.[28]

In one of his first official functions after his inauguration, President Bush addressed a group of American teachers and reminded them of his campaign pledge that he wished to be known as the education president. He told his audience that "education is the key to our very competitiveness in the future as a nation and to our very soul as a people."[29] But by summer 1989 the Bush administration had not proposed policies consistent with its concern and stated intent. He has proposed a $441 million program to reward schools that demonstrate excellence in a variety of areas, including combating drug use. More than half of the new money would go to reward schools that had educated their students particularly well as determined by improvement in test scores and decline in dropouts. The president's proposals also included $25 million to help urban schools combat drugs. The token nature of the proposals is suggested by the fact that the administration is simultaneously recommending $361 million for new prison spaces.

The overall proposed education budget is at about the same level as the last year of the Reagan administration. No changes are proposed in the major educational programs. The proposals are hardly intended to bring about significant educational improvement as a consequence of federal initiatives and are in reality so modest and uncoordinated as to be regarded as but token efforts to acknowledge campaign rhetoric.

The traditional federal role summarized well by former Secretary Bell does not address the issues facing the nation. An essentially supportive, assisting, helping, nonintrusive, ad hoc reactive federal policy is today hardly commensurate to the needs of the nation as it approaches the threshold of an uncertain and troubled twenty-first century. Has the existing pattern of educational governance adequately dealt with the educational problems so voluminously described by the score of analytical national studies that document our concern and unease? One distinguished scholar summed it up as follows: "Our difficulties are the result of expanded social problem solving in a distinctively decentralized and divided political system."[30]

Chapter 2 has sought to trace selectively the history of the federal government's involvement in public education. Although a number of attempts have been made over the course of the nation's history to hammer out a more proactive and responsible national role in education, tradition, group interests, and persistent academic antipathy toward government involvement in education have effectively precluded significant changes in the governance structures. With "governance" categorically excluded from the dialogue, issues dealing with marginal changes in schools and schooling dominate the reform debate.

In the absence of a national public policy process, important decisions affecting the country's educational processes are made by a nonpublic network of individuals and institutions. Chapter 3 attempts to define and analyze this nonpublic process, drawing attention both to the many contributions made by what we have termed "para-private" institutions and to the inherent limitations of this uniquely American approach to a national educational system.

The little fundamental reform that has occurred since the publication of *A Nation at Risk*, and the spate of other major studies that followed in its wake, has taken place at the state level. Generally these reforms have involved an improvement in accountability, which in turn has been secured by enhancing the authority of states and lessening that of local governments. Enhanced accountability has been obtained by an expansion of state curriculum requirements, increased state testing of teachers and students, a tightening of academic standards, state-imposed salary systems, and additional planning and related accountability measures.

There is some evidence that these measures have indeed led to some improvements in educational outcomes, although it is argued by some that what we are observing is simply an improved capability in rote learning, obtained by state-inspired "teaching to the test." It is also suggested that the interest of many state governors in education is probably a fickle and fleeting affair that will pass as soon as the political mileage dissipates. It is important to remind ourselves that ours is still an aging population and that in many states fewer than one third of the voters have children in the public schools. Political support for increased educational expenditure is sensitively dependent on whether the economy is churning out new revenues sufficient to permit increased expenditure for the education of other people's children without necessarily detracting from the existing level of services provided to a politically potent senior citizenry. Governors and state legislators, if they are to stay in office, must read these signals carefully and accurately. An analysis of where expenditure and reform are occurring reveals that they are closely identified with those states that have experienced economic growth, particularly in communications and other high-tech sectors—economies being particularly dependent on a qualitatively improved work force. Indeed, in those states where the economy is in serious trouble, educational reform tends to be more rhetorical than substantive. Therefore, it is not likely that the current level of state reform policies will persist, for they are critically dependent on economic and political trends. Possibly of even greater concern is the fact that while state initiatives are to be applauded, they do not constitute a national policy; nor are they based primarily on national needs and concerns. Thus, while states such as New Jersey, Tennessee, and Massachusetts direct increasing resources to improve and to render their respective educational systems more accountable, other states are doing little and in a few cases are actually cutting back on their efforts.

The serious 1989 revenue shortfalls that have plagued the public finances of the relatively wealthy northeastern states have already led to a significant cutback either in existing or in proposed levels of educational expenditure. In New Jersey, considered an education bellwether state, the April 1989 school budget elections resulted in a record number of defeats. New Jersey voters rejected 210 of the 553 proposed district budgets. Even communities with average family incomes in the hundreds of thousands of dollars rejected their proposed district budgets.

Chapter 3 outlines how a private, nonpublic national policy structure has evolved over the past century to fill a policy vacuum in American education.

NOTES

1. Fred G. Burke, "The New Federalism in Public Education," *Congressional Record*, 9 June 1977, H5691.

2. Ibid., H5692.

3. Quoted in Carl F. Kaestle and Marshall S. Smith, "The Federal Role in Elementary and Secondary Education, 1940–1980," *Harvard Educational Review* 52:4 (November 1982): 386.

4. The idea of cash grants to the states had been advanced considerably earlier than 1917 but not in the field of education.

5. Hugh Davis Graham, *The Uncertain Triumph: Federal Education Policy in the Kennedy and Johnson Years* (Chapel Hill: University of North Carolina Press, 1984), xviii.

6. Ibid., xv.

7. Ibid., 11–12.

8. Burke, "The New Federalism," H5692.

9. Nicholas Lemann, "The Unfinished War," *Atlantic* 262:6 (December 1988): 46.

10. See John E. Coons and Stephan D. Sugarman, *Education by Choice: The Case for Family Control* (Berkeley: University of California Press, 1978).

11. Arthur E. Wise, *Legislated Learning: The Bureaucratization of the American Classroom* (Berkeley: University of California Press, 1979).

12. Graham, *Uncertain Triumph*, 45.

13. Ibid., 62.

14. Fred G. Burke, Unpublished report prepared for Carter Transition Team, 1975, 2.

15. Ibid., 2.

16. Robert Carleson, quoted by Dennis Doyle, "Your Meager Slice of New Federalism Could Contain Delicious Options for Schools," *American School Board Journal* 169:4 (April 1982): 23.

17. Ibid.

18. Samuel I. Blumenfield, quoted in Terrel H. Bell, "Education Policy Development in the Reagan Administration," *Phi Delta Kappan* 67:7 (March 1986): 488.

19. Ibid., 487.

20. Ibid., 489.

21. Ibid.

22. Edward B. Fiske, "How Education Came to Be a Campaign Issue," *New York Times*, Education Supplement, 1988, 30.

23. Ibid.

24. Burke, "The New Federalism," H5692.

25. Jane Perlez, "The Debate on Schools—Educators Say Thrust of Cuomo Proposals Doesn't Address the Needs of Schoolhouse," *New York Times*, 12 December 1987, I:35.

26. Theodore Sizer, quoted in Perlez, "The Debate on Schools," I:35.

27. Governor of New Jersey Thomas Kean, quoted by Joseph F. Sullivan, "Program to Aid Troubled Youths: Jersey Schools Will Offer Counseling on Drug Abuse and Family Problems," *New York Times*, 10 January 1988, I:27.

28. Bell, "Education Policy Development," 493, emphasis added.

29. Richard L. Berke, "Bush's Domestic Policy Team Is All Set, But Not the Agenda," *New York Times*, 18 January 1989, I:1.

30. David K. Cohen, "Policy and Organization:The Impact of State and Federal Educational Policy on School Governance," *Harvard Educational Review* 52:4 (November 1982): 486.

3

A Para-Private Policy Process

Simply to advance the notion that an informal nonpublic network of individuals and institutions, in the absence of a national public process, significantly influences educational policy in the United States is to state the obvious. But the point of view advanced here is not thought to be so obvious or mundane. The individuals and institutions included in this network constitute a conscious and relatively efficient process for identifying and articulating educational issues of national import, as well as for aggregating the human, institutional, and fiscal resources necessary to formulate and implement (and just as important, for not formulating or implementing) fundamental national educational policy.

The purpose of this analysis is meant to be neither critical nor supportive of this unique policy process. Nor is it based on the premise that such a structure and process is inherently dysfunctional. Indeed, it can be argued that a nation bereft of a process for publicly making national educational policy is fortunate to have in place an effective private policy process. Having said this, however, it is necessary to add that this process is inherently limited in its capacity to raise major policy issues. By its constituent nature, it must accommodate itself to an extraordinary degree of collective consensus—a level of constituent consensus that all but precludes the likelihood of achieving fundamental reform.

COMPOSITION OF THE PARA-PRIVATE
POLICY PROCESS

The blandness and absence of proposals for educational reform commensurate with the scope and magnitude of the problems raised by the many "reports"—what one critic referred to as "weak arguments, poor data, simplistic recommendations"—are inherent in this uniquely American educational policy process.[1] Regardless of whether a given task force, commission, or study group is initiated by a foundation, by an association, or by corporate or educational leaders, it will almost certainly be composed of a cast of individuals, well known to one another, who most likely have worked together on a number of similar occasions. Predictably the cast of participants will represent the major interests, associations, and institutions generally recognized to hold fundamentally different points of view as to what needs to be changed but, nonetheless, possessed of a surprising degree of consensus as to what may not be changed. Thus, the process begins with an unspoken, but nonetheless mutually perceived, understanding that whereas there is considerable room for sweeping and even radical rhetoric, there is little leeway for fundamental change. To this limitation one must also add the fact that the recommendations, by and large, are those of a private process and therefore do not carry the weight of public authority. Tom Wicker, commenting in the *New York Times* on David Gardner's observation that the recommendations of *A Nation at Risk* would be "compelling and mostly unanimous," perceptively wrote that the document would "be binding on no one, owing to the fact that there are 16,000 public school districts, plus thousands of private and parochial schools, a vast mosaic that precludes anything like a national educational policy."[2]

It is hardly surprising that in the absence of the development of a public process for making national educational policy that a private system gradually evolved. It is difficult and somewhat arbitrary, however, to pinpoint exactly when and which individuals and institutions, in response to what were increasingly perceived as national educational needs, coalesced and gradually came to constitute what we have termed a "para-private" policy process. Certainly the founding of the NEA in 1857 might well mark such a watershed. However, for our purposes we will commence with the important contributions made by Charles Eliot, president of Harvard University from 1869 to 1909. This is not an arbitrary choice, for as this and subsequent chapters detail, it is not possible to comprehend the evolution and historic role of this nation's unique para-private educational policy process without frequent reference to key persons and events associated with Harvard University.

The evolution of a philosophy of educational governance is not necessarily the product of a deliberate and planned strategy. More likely, a consistent, fundamental point of view as to what the bedrock purposes of public education should be and who should be responsible for proclaiming such verities and for overseeing their integrity evolves over many years and is the product of many minds and events. Such a philosophy undoubtedly consists of a mosaic of numerous refinements, additions, and occasionally some recantations and retractions. But whereas it is rarely possible to attribute fundamental philosophy—especially as it has evolved over more than half a century—to a single individual, it is useful to show how that point of view was shaped by the thoughts and interactions of persons associated with one academic institution. Fundamental ideas about public education, and its impact on the well-being and destiny of the nation, have been closely associated with Harvard University for more than a century. The basic ideas that shaped this philosophy are important, for Harvard's extraordinary influence on public education in the United States is, in important part, a product of more than a half century of recruiting, educating, and then carefully placing its graduates.

ROLE OF HARVARD'S PRESIDENT CHARLES ELIOT

By the turn of the century the United States had already sensed its manifest destiny, and Harvard, the country's preeminent university, quite naturally took upon itself a share of the responsibility for helping define the nation's purposes and for guiding it along the proper path toward its destiny.

Charles Eliot was keenly aware that a great nation must identify its talented youth wherever they were to be found and provide them with a public education that would ensure that the nation's elite be academically and ethically prepared to culminate its learning at Harvard or at the nation's other, albeit somewhat lesser, institutions. President Eliot sensed that a rapidly growing and increasingly complex and sophisticated nation would require an expanding supply of well-educated secondary school graduates. He realized the critical importance of an educated and sizable middle class if the nation was to staff adequately its rapid industrialization and expanding social and political systems. Thus, the country's secondary schools, in his view, would be required to take on responsibility for identifying and preparing potentially able young Americans who could, with proper education, fill these important roles. An additional responsibility of Eliot's proposed system of secondary schools was that of separating out the most talented of all, who would go on to institutions of higher education.

From the very outset the importance of testing as a determinant of one's intelligence and likely academic capability—and thus by inference, one's intended station in life—was an integral and key element in Eliot's educational philosophy, one shared by many of his then and future associates at Harvard. Indeed, testing emerged as a key strategy in the evolving para-private national educational policy process. Testing became the technology increasingly looked to by Eliot and his colleagues to enable public education to predict, and thus in effect to proscribe, social class and status. Eliot, and those who succeeded him, argued that this educational philosophy based on an equalitarian meritocracy was in the best tradition of the nation's founding ideals. Largely overlooked, however, was the strong likelihood that the criteria associated with entry into the "better" class are as much derived from ascribed status as from educational prowess. Thus, an educational philosophy dependent in large part on testing to determine who goes to which school for how long is in effect a turnstile into the middle class or, as is increasingly evident in contemporary America, into a "permanent underclass" as well.

President Eliot was firmly convinced that the attainment of national grandeur was denied by the deplorable state of the nation's secondary schools. He lamented the lack of rigorous uniform standards, which, in his view, were a direct consequence of the near state of anarchy and the absence of professionalism that characterized American secondary public education. These concerns led him to propose to the 1890 NEA convention that a national committee be appointed to identify rigorously the problems besetting secondary education and, more important, to develop a structure and curriculum that could, and hopefully would, be nationally applicable. The resultant Committee of Ten was the first comprehensive—and in the view of some, the best—study of secondary education ever undertaken. More important for our purposes is that President Eliot and his Committee of Ten established the prototype and the precedent for a continuous series of para-private committees, studies, and reports that over the past century have effectively drawn the blueprints defining national educational policy.

Not surprisingly, President Eliot was appointed to head this important committee, and despite an elusive consensus, it was he who all but single-handedly put together the final report, a document that fundamentally shaped and continues to influence secondary education in the United States. William Harrison, one of the country's early commissioners of education, in a pattern frequently replicated by his successors, accepted membership on this private committee whose self-appointed task was explicitly, and seemingly without any question as to public accountability, to restructure the nation's system of public secondary education completely. And well it might have been.

On the basis of Eliot's report the newly established Carnegie Foundation concluded that all American high schools should adopt the sixteen Carnegie unit program. The proposed curriculum was laid out in detail, as was the recommended form of instruction. It was hardly coincidental that the curriculum was drawn primarily from that proposed earlier by Eliot and the College Education Examination Board. Commissioner Harrison concluded that Eliot's report was "the most important educational document ever published in this country."[3] However, it is important to draw attention to the fact that this landmark and precedent-setting document, which essentially determined the structure and curriculum of American secondary education, was not the product of a public policy process but rather the product of a self-appointed elite trained to believe that it "knew best what was best" for the nation.

Concerned about the implications of the variable standards that characterized the nation's thousands of relatively autonomous high schools to the needs of an increasingly national society and economy, Eliot advocated that some form of national examination be required for entry into the nation's institutions of higher education. Having identified a national educational need, the next step for Eliot and his colleagues was to come up with an institutional solution: a para-private institution. With the financial assistance of the Carnegie Corporation, Eliot was instrumental in the establishment, in 1899, of the College Entrance Examination Board. As we will have an opportunity to note, the creation of the CEEB was but the first in a succession of para-private institutions that provided the inspiration, organizational basis, resource base, and governance for the likes of Educational Testing Services (ETS) that were to follow. Nowhere else in the world is the educational and thus the future status of children and youth entrusted to tests and standards determined, devised, and often administered by private organizations.

Eliot was also instrumental in the establishment of the Carnegie Foundation for the Advancement of Teaching and in 1905 became the first chairman of its board. Convinced that an entrenched elderly faculty effectively precluded the development of more professionally oriented curricula in the nation's leading universities, and firmly believing that this was exactly what the national interest required, President Eliot sought and obtained funding from the Carnegie board to be granted to leading universities to enable them to pension off recalcitrant faculty. In retrospect it is conceivable that the incorporation of the relatively specialized professional studies and associated academic structures patterned on those of Prussia was indeed in the best interests of American universities and colleges. It can also be argued that the subsidy of faculty pensions by private philanthropic organizations was an appropriate function of the newly established Carnegie Foundation. However, the significance of this event, for our purposes, is that it starkly demonstrates the way in which a nonpublic educational policy process consisting of an intimate interlocking network of universities, foundations, and related subsidiary para-private institutions was established and exerted extraordinary influence on American education.

ROLE OF PRESIDENT JAMES CONANT

James Conant, Harvard's president from 1933 to 1953, although differing in important respects with the educational philosophy of his predecessor, was equally convinced that Harvard had a historic obligation to put its enormous resources at the disposal of the nation as it addressed the problems besetting public education. If anything, President Conant was even more convinced than was President Eliot that the primary function of the public schools was to aggregate the nation's human talents at an early age with the express purpose of "sifting and sorting" them into what Eliot referred to as "their probable destiny."[4]

Conant shared with Eliot the view that a national purpose and appropriate philosophy of education were requisite to the country's welfare. As early as the 1930s, Conant exhibited a keen interest in the CEEB and in the Scholastic Aptitude Test (SAT) that it had developed. However, the proliferation of examining and testing institutions, and of curriculum and standard establishing boards—

many launched by the Harvard "school"—was perceived to detract from a more focused and thus more effective effort. It was with this concern in mind that President Conant in 1947 spearheaded a successful effort to consolidate aspects of the CEEB, the Carnegie Foundation for the Advancement of Teaching, and the American Council on Education to spin off the ETS. Not surprisingly, Henry Chauncey, the first and long-tenured chairman of the ETS, was a Harvard associate of Conant's. In the 1930s, at Conant's encouragement, Chauncey had worked on the development of scholastic testing programs.

It is difficult to conceive of an institution that exerts greater influence on American education than the ETS. Since its inception from the brainstorming of Conant and his Harvard colleagues, it has grown into a multimillion dollar enterprise that uniquely and powerfully affects the educational destiny of the nation's youth and thus the nation's destiny as well.

The focus for Harvard's near-century-long concern with national educational policy has tended to center in either the office of the president or in the Graduate School of Education. It was Eliot who established the Department of Teacher Training, which subsequently evolved into Harvard's renowned Graduate School of Education. Throughout his long career in American education Conant often questioned the efficacy of graduate schools of education. He consistently expressed the view that public education was far too important to be left to the self-interests of the educational establishment. He advocated, albeit unsuccessfully, that teacher education and certification be put in the hands of a university-wide committee, not only at Harvard but throughout the nation as well. This of course would have effectively removed teacher certification from the public sector and placed it in the hands of a para-private process.

Conant was primarily responsible for the development of Harvard's Masters of Arts/Teaching (MAT) degree, a program that, with Ford Foundation support, has been emulated by many of the nation's leading universities.

Conant's career has spanned much of the nation's contemporary educational history. This scholar, university president, ambassador, and educational spokesperson extraordinaire influenced American educational thought and policy more profoundly than any person since Horace Mann. For nearly half a century his was a position to be reckoned with in American education, a position that stamped its values and ideas firmly on the national fabric. Unfortunately, he shared with many of his contemporaries a near blindness to this nation's "Third World." In his later years, as the country's minority, non-English-speaking, poor children grew from a tiny minority to a near majority, his philosophy of meritocracy as the highway to a more equalitarian, intellectual, and sophisticated America became increasingly divorced from the stark realities of the times.

Conant, like many of us, was a product of the Great Depression, World War II, and then the cold war. As such, he was inclined to see the world accordingly. The specter of massive unemployment, particularly of a disaffected black minority, and of a looming Soviet military and scientific menace, increasingly shaped his views of the purposes and thus the requirements of the nation's schools and universities.

Even during his sojourn as first high commissioner and then ambassador to West Germany (1953–57) he brooded and anguished over the state of America's educational enterprise and pondered ways and means to work its salvation, all in the national interest as he perceived it. Even before returning from Germany, Ambassador Conant was busy negotiating with the Carnegie Foundation for funds to support still another major study of American secondary education.

Given the now firmly established network of relationships and thus of the essentially shared views and concerns noted above, it followed quite naturally that Ambassador Conant would receive a substantial grant from the Carnegie Foundation to carry out his mission of overhauling the nation's high schools. Not surprisingly, arrangements were made for this grant to be administered by the ETS, one of the more recent spin-offs of the nation's para-private educational policy process. The purpose of the grant was to enable Conant to undertake a comprehensive study of American high schools—not unlike that of his Harvard predecessor more than a half century earlier.

Despite the flow of years and events, Conant retained his conviction that the fundamental purpose of the nation's high schools was to "sift and sort" to identify and to process the nation's intellectual resources according to their intended station in life. His monumental study emphasized the importance of the high school to the attainment by all American youth of an understanding and appreciation of the nation's common culture and citizenship. He also advocated that economically relevant job skills be made available for those "unable," for whatever reason, to aspire to the higher stations in life. But his major concern was with the capacity of the nation's secondary schools to provide adequately for those who demonstrated that they were prepared and able to cope with advanced academic subjects.

Heading up the Carnegie Foundation at this important point in time when Conant was seeking resources to revamp the nation's secondary school systems was John Gardner, a close friend of Conant's and a person who in his own right was playing an increasingly important role in the evolution of a national, albeit para-private, educational policy. In 1960 Gardner took time from his foundation responsibilities to head up the Kennedy Task Force on Education and again in 1964 to chair Lyndon Johnson's White House Conference on Education. In 1965 President Johnson appointed him secretary of HEW. Secretary Gardner, in turn, designated Harold Howe III as U.S. Commissioner of Education.

Conant shared Eliot's early concerns as to whether the traditional educational establishment had either the capacity or the inclination to deal with the enormous problems that he perceived were facing the nation's schools. Like Eliot, he also believed that wherever the solution to the nation's educational problems happened to lie, it was certainly not with the public sector. Conant exemplified the prevalent university/academic philosophy that government was at best bureaucratically stultifying and at worst corrupt and inherently politically partisan. But if this were indeed the frightful state of educational affairs, where should those who had the noblesse oblige to worry about the nation's schools turn for support? Two strategies were pursued. On the one hand, the public should be mobilized primarily at the most local and thus pristine level of all, the community: "The road to better schools will be paved by the collective action of the local citizenry in thousands of communities. The responsibility for the sorely needed upgrading of our schools cannot be passed to the state legislatures or to the Congress."[5]

The second strategy involved entrusting responsibility for framing key educational issues and proposed policies to the para-private network that both Presidents Eliot and Conant had done so much over the years to establish. This dual strategy persists as the mainstay of national educational policy-making in the United States.

The tenacious inclination of the educational establishment—whether in a university, foundation, or association—to revere community democracy and to suspect public authority regardless of how democratically legitimized is an important factor shaping the current debate on educational governance and reform.

The stream of influential Conant studies and reports that shaped the structure and essence of American education for half a century were consistent: They were supported by the Carnegie Foundation or by one of its derivatives and uniformly extolled the virtues of community control and conversely warned against the evils of state and federal involvement—interestingly enough, all in the national interest.

In 1964, some thirty years after his first profound comments on the nation's educational woes, Ambassador Conant, in one of his last words, *Shaping Educational Policy*, again sought a formula that would bridge the pristine virtues of a Grandma Moses–like local control: community democracy and the increasingly obvious need for a national educational policy.[6] To be consistent with the liturgy, such a formula would have to be at the same time local and community oriented but designed and led by a national nonpublic para-private institution. His solution was to suggest, in 1964, the creation of "a commission for planning a national educational policy." He advocated that the proposed commission be composed of distinguished persons from each of the states but that they not be recruited from the ranks of professional educators. A commission, as proposed by Conant with the support of Gardner in his capacity as president of the Carnegie Foundation, was duly established as the Education Commission of the States (ECS), a para-private institution that shares its birthmark with the ETS, the CEEB, the American Council on Education, and so on.

The essence of a national educational policy capability, according to Conant and his colleagues, is well established: It should seek necessary public support from a helter-skelter of thousands of local communities; whenever possible it should avoid the involvement of state and federal governments; it should elicit its ideas and support from a university community with ties into foundations and centers with available financial resources; and it should be headed by fellow members of the para-private network.

THE HARVARD LEGACY

If the Eliot/Conant mantle has been passed, it probably is now with Harold Howe III, Senior Lecturer, Harvard Graduate School of Education. Howe's many and influential commentaries on education and youth consistently draw attention to the complexity, the national dimensions, and the multifaceted nature of the issues. However, in common with nearly all his colleagues, his numerous and influential former students, and his many strategically placed protégés, he is inclined to ignore the long and persistent failure of the nation's decentralized education system but consistently warns against the dangers and folly of anything other than a narrow and limited role for the federal government. Although he is keenly aware of the inadequacies of the existing system, he prefers remedies that would further decentralize education to the community and school building levels. His solution to the need to develop increased national coordination and policy initiatives is consistent with that of his illustrious predecessors: establish an additional para-private institution. For example, in 1987 he suggested that consideration be given to the development of what he terms a "National Children's Center" to be composed essentially of representatives of various private educational interest groups. Subsequently, Howe was named to head a new para-private national commission funded by the William T. Grant Foundation. Samuel Halprin, who was Assistant U.S. Commissioner of Education under Howe and later the second director of the Institute for Educational Leadership, until recently chaired by Howe, was appointed to head the commission's important study "The Forgotten Half: Non-College Youth in America."[7]

Harvard's James Conant, as with Howe, was also inclined, on the one hand, to advocate the imperative of pursuing a national agenda to secure a more uniform policy while, on the other hand, fervently cautioning against the instrumentality of the federal government to address acknowledged national needs. A quarter of a century ago he warned his countrymen that "educational policy in the United States has been determined in the past by the more or less haphazard interaction of (1) . . . public school teachers, administrators, and professors of education, (2) state educational authorities, (3) a multitude of state colleges and universities."[8] He concluded that the existing governance process was chaotic and needed to be changed. But, as with Howe, he did not therefore conclude that a public national policy process was required— possibly a nationwide policy but certainly not a national policy: "All this does not add up to a nation wide educational policy, let alone a national educational policy. . . . We cannot have a national educational policy, but we might be able to evolve a nation wide educational policy."[9] His strategy for achieving the latter and avoiding the former, as noted above, involved the establishment of the Education Commission of the States, an influential institution but one limited essentially to making recommendations to state and local authorities.

The views of two of Harvard's more eminent sons, Harold Howe III and James Conant, are presented here to draw attention to their shared philosophical positions on educational governance: a consistent disinclination to resort to a national public policy process as a desirable or logical vehicle to resolve acknowledged grave national educational problems, while being more inclined to turn to the creation of an overlapping network of para-private institutions.

PARA-PRIVATE PROCESS IN OPERATION

An important consequence of this historical antipathy toward a major policy role for the federal government consistent with the magnitude and scope of the national crisis is to cast the reform issues in narrow school/schooling parameters, which in turn acts to assign the analysis of these matters to school- and schooling-oriented academics, interest groups, and professionals. Thus, it is not surprising that the numerous reform commissions essentially limited their recommendations to marginal changes in the schools and in the working conditions and rewards of educators. This insensitivity to the national dimensions of the country's educational and, more important, its youth problems, accompanied by a disinclination to look to national political processes and institutions for a solution, has also acted to encourage the proliferation of para-private processes and institutions to address what are acknowledged to be national issues. This prevailing philosophy, which has effectively argued against a proactive role for the national government, has persisted for nearly a century and has been nurtured and promulgated by generations of scholars, leaders of key foundations, and educational associations, most frequently associated with Harvard University and often flowing in and out of major educational positions in state and federal governments.

Eliot's turn-of-the-century Committee of Ten (which fundamentally restructured the nation's system of secondary education), the College Entrance Examination Board, the Carnegie Foundation for the Advancement of Teaching, the Educational Testing Services, the Education Commission of the States, the American Council on Education, the Institute for Educational Leadership, and most recently, the National Board for Professional Teaching Standards (NBPTS) are all essentially products of this process and together constitute a para-private national educational policy process that in nearly all other countries is provided by agencies of national and state governments.

The recent development of the NBPTS illustrates well the manner in which this para-private policy process works. Established in 1987, the NBPTS grew out of recommendations included in a report entitled *A Nation Prepared: Teachers for the 21st Century*, commissioned by the Carnegie Forum on Education and the Economy. The Carnegie Foundation granted nearly a million dollars to the National Governors Association to facilitate altering state certification and teacher training policies to conform to those recommended by the Carnegie Forum. The logic is consistent. It commences with an assumption that the existing state-by-state process for certifying teachers varies erratically from one state to another and therefore is no longer adequate to serve national requirements. What is required is a more comprehensive national approach but not one that requires involvement of the public sector. The operational response is the creation of another para-private institution. The majority of the members of NBPTS, this potentially powerful private institution, are teachers. The initial composition of the board was augmented with the appointment of thirty-four additional members. James A. Kelly, formerly with the Ford Foundation, was appointed president. The NBPTS, which obtained its initial funding of $1 million from the Carnegie Foundation, is developing a set of teacher certification standards and intends to issue a national teaching certificate by 1993 to those who meet the qualifications and make proper application. Although NBPTS certification, by definition, cannot be nationally mandatory, its impact on American education is potentially as pervasive as are the major programs of other para-private institutions such as the ETS and the CEEB. It is likely that a number of states, urged by the para-private network, will authoritatively adopt NBPTS certification. Once again, a network of para-private institutions in no way accountable to the public will in effect be determining the nation's educational future.

Albert Shanker, president of the National Federation of Teachers and a strong supporter of the NBPTS, is of the opinion that over time this privately construed and awarded teaching certificate will provide educators with "the same professional autonomy" as doctors and lawyers.[10] However, President Shanker overlooks an important distinction: With few exceptions, doctors and lawyers operate within the private sector, whereas most teachers are public servants.

This uniquely American process for making fundamental decisions about public education has been treated in some detail, for along with the federal structure of our political system and a pervasive tradition of local control, it helps explain the ineffectiveness of a decade of educational reform and a failure to deal with the national trauma of youth in crisis. Chapter 4 is concerned with this neglected and endangered population of Americans.

NOTES

1. Lawrence C. Steadman and Marshall S. Smith, "Weak Arguments, Poor Data, Simplistic Recommendations," in *The Great School Debate: Which Way for American Education?*, ed. Beatrice Gross and Ronald Gross (New York: Simon and Schuster, 1985), 85.

2. Tom Wicker, "Our Troubled Schools," *New York Times*, 29 March 1983, I:21.

3. Commissioner Harrison, quoted in Henry J. Perkinson, *200 Years of American Educational Thought* (New York: University Printers of America, 1976), 153.

4. Ibid., 242.

5. Ibid., 253.

6. James Bryant Conant, *Shaping Educational Policy* (New York: McGraw-Hill, 1964), 128–31.

7. William T. Grant Foundation Commission on Work, Family, and Citizenship, *The Forgotten Half: Non-College-Bound Youth in America* (Washington, D.C.: William T. Grant Foundation, 1988), 196.

8. Conant, *Shaping Educational Policy*, 109.

9. Ibid., 110.

10. Albert Shanker, quoted in Dennis Hevesi, "Board Named to Set Teacher Standards," *New York Times*, 16 May 1987, I:9.

4

A Generation at Risk

The crisis facing the nation is less one of "education" than it is of a troubled "youth." The preoccupation of a decade of reform with the educational crisis is the product of the peculiar nature of educational governance and policy-making that is characteristic of the United States.

The absence of a public process for making national educational policy, combined with the tenacity of a philosophy of local control, in effect has defaulted national educational decision making to a network of private foundations, academia, and related professional associations—a network that perceives of the crisis as one essentially limited to schools and schooling. The net effect of this policy process is a reform strategy preoccupied with marginal changes in school structure and teacher quality. This enthrallment with school and schooling reform tends to ignore the need for more fundamental systemic changes that might conceivably address the more comprehensive and important issue of youth in crisis.

ISOLATION OF SCHOOL FROM SOCIETY

A frequently overlooked consequence of the unique degree of local control that characterizes American education is the tendency to isolate educational functions and institutions from the larger society. Although Americans have always perceived education as critical to preparing successive generations for fruitful participation in society, we nonetheless have tended to isolate school and schooling from the very activity for which they supposedly ready the nation's youth. In recent years a number of scholars have commented on the growing discrepancy between what school teaches and what life on "the outside" requires. Schools are inclined to teach generalities and abstractions, whereas the workaday world puts a premium on the specific and the concrete. The student is evaluated on the basis of individual performance, whereas the employee is judged according to his or her ability to function effectively in a group.[1]

During the depression, in order for this writer to get to and from his four-room school it was necessary to walk past the swinging doors of the "saloon," past the "general store," which also served as a warm place for the high school students to wait for the bus, past the town clerk's office and the blacksmith shop, where if time permitted, and sometimes even if it did not, we might be asked to pump the bellows, past the feed mill and the railway depot. Much of what we would need to know and be able to do to one day take our places in the community was experienced firsthand on a regular basis. But as American society has become more socially and economically complex, we have increasingly been inclined to build our schools, and especially our secondary schools, in isolated, remote, often rural locations where we daily transport tomorrow's citizenry in generationally segregated buses. These young people, for the greater part of the day, are effectively shielded from the reality for which at great expense they supposedly are being prepared. This segregation of the educational enterprise from societal realities also inclines educators in its employ to become obsessively possessive of their prerogatives: Education should be left to educators, for only they understand the pedagogical needs and generational idiosyncrasies of the nation's youth with whom they are of necessity exclusively closeted for a goodly portion of their respective lives. Thus, education is increasingly portrayed as an art form, with the children as the canvas and the teachers as artists; it is not for outsiders to comprehend or indeed to question the process or product of this isolated artistic creativity. This relative isolation tends invariably to render "learning to become" a peculiarly vicarious activity obtained secondhand, either through two-dimensional textbooks or through the necessarily selective sieve of the teacher's own experience and biases. It also disinclines those responsible for the enterprise from casting it in an enlarged, more relevant milieu.

Ironically it is the nation's problematic urban schools attempting to serve a troubled generation of predominantly minority American children and youth that are relatively integrated into their immediate social and economic milieus. Historically the proximity of urban schools to the vibrant economy and society that was once characteristic of most cities helps explain their once-heralded academic preeminence. But today's inner-city neighborhoods are rarely distinguished by either economic opportunity or civic pride. Paradoxically the easy access that urban schools provide to their immediate environs, rather than furthering the ideal integration of schooling and society, provides inner-city youth with a persistent and powerful cultural reality that is in marked contrast to that of mainstream Americans. The society for which urban schools are supposedly preparing their students is today as far removed from reality as is that of the isolated suburban school.

Historically efforts to expand education beyond the parochial parameters of an existent time or place were opposed by those in control of the enterprise as a dangerous denial of local control and as a threat to "their" children. Those advocating a more centralized system have tended to rest their case on the emergent requirements of an increasingly regional and national society, that all children, at least to a point, be uniformly socialized. Certainly both values are in flux and are fundamental to American culture and history. A national centralized system of education might well serve countries such as France, possessed of a long history of national dominance. However, few would argue that such a system is either feasible or desirable for the United States. But it is equally evident that the extraordinary scope and pace of change make it imperative that education, in its broadest sense, further vital national interests as well as those of the parochial community. The key issue facing the nation today is whether it is possible to conceive and implement changes in the overall educational system to ensure that the national interests are addressed, while preserving the essence of the traditional governance structure. More time and energy need to be devoted to addressing this issue boldly than to concluding categorically that "what is must forever be as it is." The nation has witnessed a persistent struggle as to the locus of educational authority.

The concern of the turn-of-the-century WASP (white Anglo-Saxon Protestant) establishment with the tidal wave of "swarthy, Polish" immigrants contributed much to successful efforts to wrest control over the education of their children from the highly politicized urban wards and ghettos. Historically centralization of educational governance has been strategically employed by the dominant power structure to ensure that who teaches what to whom to what end conforms to its values. The resultant centralization of education to the district level at the turn of the century was accompanied by professionalization of the educational bureaucracy. The establishment argued that consolidation of education to the district level would remove school governance from the sordid hands of urban politicians by entrusting the management of the enterprise to a newly emergent breed of professional, "apolitical" educational administrators. Thus, what was initially perceived as a strategy to ensure that the schools would properly socialize immigrant youth acted to isolate effectively schools and schooling from the immediate social and political realities of life.

The educational establishment has traditionally resisted changes. Whereas emergent classes and ethnic groups, in the saga that is America, gradually wrested considerable political influence away from the WASP establishment, the fiction that education was apolitical and therefore properly the exclusive prerogative of expert professionals, benignly overviewed by an equally apolitical "old establishment," served to perpetuate the isolation of schools and schooling from society.

The tenacious factional issue of who controls the schools and for what purpose, sparked by the civil rights movement and Johnson's War on Poverty, erupted again in the 1960s. This time, however, the ball was in the court of those seeking to wrest control away from what was perceived to be an alien remote central bureaucracy in order to return it to the community, where it "rightfully" belonged. The nation's academicians and foundations, not surprisingly, were in the forefront of this "populist" crusade.

The New York City school system provides a timely illustration. The racial confrontation that characterized the 1960s spilled over into the schools in New York City, as it did elsewhere in the nation. Advocates of the black and Hispanic communities, many of whom came from the ranks of liberal academia, argued that the white-dominated city board of education and the teachers' union perpetuated a system that was perceived to be both racist and educationally flawed. In 1970 the state legislature, reacting to a protracted period of racial hostility and massive teacher strikes, voted to decentralize the New York City system by constituting thirty-two "community districts."

Kenneth Clark the eminent black social scientist, was at the time a member of the New York State Board of Regents. Not surprisingly, he was a leading and powerful advocate for the decentralization of the school system to the community level. Two decades later he is not so sure that decentralization was the way to go: "I was all for decentralization until I saw how it was being abused. I thought that parents would play a significant role in the schools. They have not. They have been blocked out by the politicians and the school unions. I don't see any benefits from decentralization."[2]

In 1987 and 1988 the increasingly evident failures of the decentralized system to achieve any of its heralded goals reached crisis proportions. A grand jury heard evidence that kickbacks, bribes, and required political contributions were the price for jobs and promotions. The arrest of a school principal for the purchase and possession of cocaine, in late 1988, unloosed an avalanche of accusations and investigations. While some would argue that the problem is not with decentralization but with the flawed legislation, and while others maintain that the problem is that decentralization did not go far enough, it is abundantly clear that the nation's largest school system, a system predominantly black and Hispanic, is in a serious state of crisis. The architects of decentralization anticipated the evolution of Rousseauistic community democracies that would effectively replace the stagnant, insensitive central bureaucracy. The unions were quick to obtain influence, either directly or indirectly, on the thirty-two community boards.

That decentralization was more the romantic vision of academics and community advocates than a massive popular ground swell is suggested by the fact that less than 15 percent of the eligible voters bothered to turn out for the first board elections in 1970—a turnout that over the years has decreased to about 7 percent and in 1989, despite extraordinary efforts, to 6 percent. The parents and other members of the community simply have not behaved as planned. The problem lies less with the system's structural flaws than it does with the underlying assumptions. Community and parental support and involvement depend on the existence of a relatively stable population that associates its well-being and interests with public institutions. This sense of community and civility, which is identified with the affluent suburbs, is not well entrenched in most urban neighborhoods.

Until the more fundamental issues besieging those inhabiting the nation's urban ghettos and rural slums are effectively addressed, decentralization of responsibility and authority to the community level not only will fail to resolve education and youth problems but in all likelihood will exacerbate them, for effective decentralization to the community presupposes the presence of community.

While the New York legislature considers proposals to remove powers from corrupt, unrepresentative community boards, the

Illinois legislature, in December 1988, voted to radically decentralize governance to Chicago's 522 schools, with authority, as of
July 1989, delegated to the building level for hiring and firing,
letting contracts, and establishing much of the curriculum. Authority will be in the hands of elected parent councils composed of six
parents, two community residents, and two teachers. Principals
will no longer enjoy tenure but will have to settle for four-year
renewable contracts to be determined by the parent councils, which
will also possess authority to fill teaching vacancies. There is little
evidence that New York's tragically failed decentralization policy
has been taken into consideration. It is difficult to comprehend the
logic that leads to devolvement of policy-making and finance for
the education of children and youth to the community when all
experience points both to a record of tragic failure and to the
absence of community.

The trend to turn authority for the most fundamental issues of
public education finance, curriculum, and personnel over to local
board and councils, despite lack of evidence that decentralization,
by any measure, leads to improved schools, is currently gathering
momentum. That this trend is obtaining increasing support from
many of the nation's largest troubled urban schools systems despite
a half century of failed and corrupt community governance experiments in education as well as in other related fields is difficult to
comprehend. In Detroit the newly elected board of education is
embarking on a process of radical decentralization of decision
making and finance to the school/community level. The troubled
Boston school system has embraced an equally comprehensive
decentralization scheme. Each of the city's schools is to be governed by a "school site council" composed of administrators,
teachers, parents, members of the community, and representatives
from the corporate sector. The advocates of these various schemes
promise that education decision making, once decentralized to the
community, will bring about the desired reforms. In words and
enthusiasm reminiscent of the architects of the disastrous New
York City decentralization scheme, they attribute the debacle of
urban education to problems with school and schooling and par-

ticularly to the insensitivity of distant district and state bureaucracies. The remedy is to purge the process, to the degree possible, of all external influence and give responsibility to the teachers, parents, and the community. However, the stark absence of community in the nation's troubled inner cities is even more pronounced today than it was during the failed War on Poverty Community Action experiments of the 1960s or at the commencement of the disastrous decentralization of New York City schools. There is little reason to expect that the newly proposed councils and boards will escape the temptations of politicization and corruption.

Parental involvement, acknowledged as requisite to the success of school site decentralization, requires the presence of relatively stable families involved in the education and socialization of their children. Community responsibility, in turn, is dependent on the presence of relatively stable neighborhoods possessed of a number of effective and legitimate social/cultural institutions. Although there are instances where both a vital family structure and a sense of community characterize inner-city urban neighborhoods, this is the exception and not the rule. Experience does not support the supposition that either the parents, community members, or teachers, given the conditions that characterize most inner-city schools neighborhoods, will in substantial numbers serve the new decentralized systems, or if so, that they will do so in a disinterested manner.

Commenting on the corruption plaguing New York City's decentralized schools, a former member of the city board of education was quoted to have concluded, "It [decentralization] works in Scarsdale and it works in Winnetka. But it doesn't seem to work well in big cities, and it certainly hasn't worked . . . well, in New York City."[3]

John Chubb, formerly with the Brookings Institution and recently appointed to a key position in the U.S. Department of Education in the Bush administration, is emerging as a key spokesperson for the virtues of decentralization. In a recent piece in the *New York Times* he suggested that the major problems of urban schools were attributable to overcentralization. He espouses more parental and teacher decision making as a remedy to having organizational structures imposed on them from the outside.[4] What Chubb and a number of other academics leave out in their analysis is that the public schools are deliberately organized to conform to a structure that evolves as a product of the public policy process designed to ensure the public that the education of the state's children is in the public interest. It is not possible to reform American education by making the public schools over in the guise of private schools governed by an association of parents, teachers, and select community members. Public schools exist not only to provide a basic education but to ensure the larger community that the products of these schools are able and inclined to contribute to and assume responsibility for the commonweal. How is it possible to accommodate the educational requirements of the United States as the nation embarks on the uncertainties of the twenty-first century if what is taught, by whom, how, to what purpose, and how well are determined by hundreds of thousands of publicly unaccountable school/community councils? Surely the nation deserves more than this!

On those few occasions in the nation's history when it seemed as if a more comprehensive approach than "schooling" would be necessary to address the changing needs of the nation's youth properly, the tenacious isolation of the public schools from social and economic realities inclined national policy to strategically circumvent the public education system. Periodic attempts to develop a national youth policy, in an environment dominated by local control and states' rights, illustrate well the circumvention strategies that of necessity are employed whenever the federal government seeks to address these issues.

EFFORTS TO DEVELOP A NATIONAL YOUTH POLICY

The establishment in 1912 of the Children's Bureau in the federal government is suggestive of an inclination to view the needs of youth as being broader than just education. The Johnson administration's determination to deal systemically with issues of poverty and inequality led it to embrace a child, as opposed to an education, strategy. Secretary of HEW Joseph Califano, who had the vision to see beyond traditional categorical boundaries, was a strong advocate of a policy that would address the broader issues concerning the welfare of the nation's children and youth. In 1966 his advocacy of this strategy led to the presidentially appointed Hunt Task Force on Child Development, composed primarily of eminent scholars from a number of the nation's leading universities. This task force report, like many of its predecessors, was boldly conceived and innovative, but it was also politically naive and thus fatally flawed. Commenting on this political naïveté, Hugh Davis Graham remarked that "the report's leading structural recommendation sounded starkly Orwellian; establish a Federal Office for Children in the DHEW, administered by an officer . . . equivalent in rank to the chief officers for health, education, and welfare."[5]

Consistent with the Community Action philosophy that characterized the early years of Johnson's War on Poverty, the Hunt Task Force proposals to provide comprehensive services to the nation's youth involved funding a bewildering array of existing and proposed community agencies and groups. Ironically proposals to empower neighborhood community organizations came at a time when the highly decentralized administration of other Great Society policies had already begun to raise serious questions as to their efficacy and propriety. The overall dismal record of what was deemed to be a "democratic user-oriented" approach did little to elicit political support from Congress or, for that matter, from the local establishment. Although the architects of the Great Society correctly realized the necessity of circumventing the educational establishment and its more than 16,000 parochial institutions, they nonetheless sought to decentralize further program management to newly established, supposedly more representative and democratic local power structures. Predictably the educational establishment was not enthusiastic about this circumvention. Nolan Estes, long an insightful observer of the macroeducation scene, commented on the Hunt proposals in a typical manner:

[T]he failure to give the schools adequate mention reflects the perennial problem of trying, on the one hand to strengthen the role of the school in the community, and on the other by-passing it because it won't perform in the specific manner desired. . . . The fundamental question here is, who is to authoritatively determine 'the specific manner desired' and for what societal end or purpose?[6]

As the Johnson administration wound down, increasingly rendered ineffective by the Vietnam War, additional task force reports advocating a comprehensive national youth policy and circumventing the educational system and establishment were forthcoming. Although they, too, came to naught, mention is made here of one such effort to illustrate further the inclination of academically staffed study groups to insist that the only legitimate role for the federal government, in this vital policy area, be limited to the provision of funds to often ad hoc and unaccountable local and community agencies. A 1968 report dealing with urban education recommended an Urban Education Services Act which would provide federal grants to Urban Education Service Agencies, local groups consisting of one or more colleges or universities, state and/or local government agencies, representative community groups, and elementary and secondary governing bodies.[7]

Despite the repeated failure of a comprehensive youth policy to survive the political wars, and the demonstrated failure of a myriad of overlapping, often mystifying, rarely accountable local and community agencies to translate federal dollars into significant and lasting reform, the dream of somehow realizing a comprehensive federal policy through the parochial efforts of thousands of quasi-independent agencies persists. By the 1980s, however, the relatively radical reform language of the 1960s and 1970s had given way to the orthodoxy of a national role limited to targeting categorical dollars to encourage and entice community agencies, states, and local school districts to move in a direction consistent with the national interest.

PREOCCUPATION WITH EDUCATIONAL REFORM

The multitude of national studies documenting *A Nation At Risk* are concerned almost exclusively with educational issues: curriculum, time on task, the length of the teaching day or year, teacher preparation, accountability, compensation, student attendance, test-measured standards, and so on. The historic isolation of schools and schooling from the realities of society is partly responsible for the limited scope of the spate of national educational studies and reports. While one occasionally finds a brief aside suggesting that the educational needs and problems afflicting the nation's inner cities are somewhat unique, most of the reform studies essentially maintain that the issue primarily concerns schools and schooling and that the remedies therefore are more or less universally applicable. Given the narrow preoccupation of the many reform studies with education, the aversion of the educational establishment to change, and the antipathy of academia to a proactive role for the federal government, it is not surprising that the solutions to a nation at risk tend to be consistently parochial, conservative, uncoordinated, and from a national point of view, nonauthoritative. This is hardly a policy process commensurate to the complexity and enormity of the "national crisis."

Except for what occurs—or better still, what does not occur—in the nation's urban ghettos and rural slums, education in the United States is *not* in crisis. If one controls for these factors, the problems of American education, as measured in the usual terms of student performance, attendance, employability, continued education, and the like, are marginal. The preponderance of the nation's schools located in middle-class environs, by most measures, are better today than they were a generation ago. Overall, relatively more high school age youngsters are enrolled, graduate, and proceed to a college or university. Declining SAT scores have stabilized and give some evidence of improvement. This is not to suggest that all is well with education in suburbia. In recent years a number of influential studies have drawn attention to the other side of the coin, for example, "cultural illiteracy," ignorance of world geography and economics, and the relatively poor academic performance of American students in contrast to those from other developed nations.

There is, nonetheless, a national crisis, one that afflicts millions of youth and children who have the misfortune of residing in the country's urban ghettos and rural backwaters. The fundamental problem facing the nation is not one of education—certainly not the education of most of our youth; rather, it is the disaffection, the despair, the ignorance, the futurelessness, the seeming relegation to a permanent underclass of the growing millions of black and Hispanic youngsters increasingly isolated from the rest of society.

The failure to comprehend the significance of this distinction is partly attributable to our preoccupation with the reform of education. Thus, we seem doomed to persistently pose the wrong questions, to which we then advance solutions that are only relevant to marginal educational problems characteristic of the implicit model: middle-class suburban schools and communities. The consequences of this inadvertent neglect of the real essence of our national trauma are enormous, and it is to this subject that we now turn our attention.

YOUTH, EDUCATION, AND A
PERMANENT UNDERCLASS

Explanations for the emergence in the United States during the later years of twentieth century of a seemingly permanent underclass are numerous and often biased and infer a variety of often conflicting policy approaches.

The growing number of Americans existing at or below the poverty line and the endless depressing scenes of the wretched and growing legion of the homeless, single-parent, and no-parent homes have spawned a series of analytical studies. Research shows not only that the number of poor has grown significantly in recent years but that the rate of increase among the poorest of the poor is substantially greater. It is these, the least fortunate of all, that are most likely to speak a language other than English and to live in the inner-city desolation of the nation's urban ghettos or rural slums, isolated by drugs, unemployment, and alienation from the mainstream of American society.

The Census Bureau recently reported that as of 1985 more than 33 million Americans—14 percent of the nation's people—were classified as poor. Approximately 18 million Hispanics live in the United States; of these, some 5.3 million, nearly one in three, live below the poverty line. For the nation's Afro-Americans the picture is equally grim; more than one in every four Americans living in poverty is black. But the category of human being most devastated by poverty is the nation's children and particularly its very young black and Hispanic urban youngsters.

The proportion of the nation's poor living in metropolitan areas increased from 62 percent of the total in 1979 to 70 percent in 1985. Indicative of the increasing concentration of the country's poor citizens residing in racially segregated ghettos is the fact that in the decade between 1970 and 1980 the proportion of poor Americans living in predominantly poverty neighborhoods nearly doubled.

Even Pope John Paul, who usually saves his homilies on poverty and equity for Third World audiences, reminded his American flock during his September 1987 visit:

> Even in this wealthy nation, committed by the Founding Fathers, to the dignity and equality of all persons, the black community suffers a disproportionate share of economic deprivation. Far too many of your young people receive less than an equal opportunity for quality education, and for gainful employment.[8]

Increasingly the poorest of the poor are children. Since 1979 the number of families, some 5.5 million of them, classified as "poor with children" has increased by more than one third. As of 1986 three of every ten children in the United States—nearly 20 million—were living in poverty, and by 1989 one in every four was born in poverty. It is estimated that there are approximately 750,000 homeless children in the United States, more than the total enrollment in all but eighteen states, and that nearly half of them do not attend school regularly. In its 1988 convention the Conference of Mayors concluded that the problems of the cities' children were escalating despite an array of highly touted teenage pregnancy, drug, and drop-out prevention programs.

Contrary to the prevailing view of the pathology of the inner city as one characterized by a historic confluence of minority residence and poverty giving rise to the plethora of problems with which we are all acquainted is the argument that this condition is a relatively recent phenomenon and thus is neither endemic nor inevitable. William Julius Wilson, author of *The Inner City and Public Policy*, reminds us that until quite recently the inner city was inhabited by black families from the entire economic spectrum.[9] However, over the past two decades the black middle class has fled the ghetto. The sociocultural and economic infrastructure did not survive this emigration. It is this important demographic change, Wilson persuasively argues, that is primarily responsible for the current pathology we associate with the nation's inner-city ghettos.[10] If one assesses the significance of the consequent concentration and thus isolation of poor black and Hispanic populations, it is possible to see beyond the generally accepted "culture of poverty" argument. This traditional interpretation attributes the inner city's ills to a long history of racial, as opposed to economic or class, isolation and accompanying poverty, which in turn have generated a distinct subculture that is highly impervious to change. This point of view inclines many educational reformers to conclude that the problem lies with the tenacious persistence of the acquired subculture, and therefore the role of the schools must be to inculcate somehow successfully the values and mores of mainstream America. Wilson, and increasingly other scholars as well, argues that it is the isolation of minority poor from economic opportunities that perpetuates the crisis. In New York City, for example, less than a quarter of the sixteen- to nineteen-year-old youths are employed or looking for a job. Each year about 125,000 young New Yorkers drop out of school, whereas the local economy generates only 26,000 jobs not requiring a high school education.

As noted above, an important implication of the nearly exclusive focus of the spate of studies and reports on schools and schooling has been to ignore relatively the critically important fact that the fundamental issue is less one of the education of America's children than it is the plight of minority American youth eking out an existence in the nation's urban and rural slums. Ernest Boyer, president of the Carnegie Foundation for the Advancement of Teaching, himself a prime mover and author of a number of influential studies, recently concluded that the educational reform process simply ignores the interests of most poor children.

THE RACE FACTOR

A major correlate, if not contributor, to the youth crisis is the magnitude of the demographic changes that have dramatically altered the ethnic composition and domicile of the nation's polyglot society over the past three decades. The American dilemma, the trauma of a nation divided by color, was eloquently chronicled by the perceptive Swedish sociologist Gunnar Myrdal.[11] The American dilemma persists as a major determinant of where and for how long we go to school, and if so, how we earn our daily bread, when and of what we die, and how many and how we raise our children. To date, our society has been unable and/or unwilling to purge itself of a legacy of racially prescribed slavery and its bequest of endemic racism and segregation. More than two decades have passed since the Kerner Commission warned that America was on the verge of becoming two societies—one black and one white, separate and unequal. The commission targeted "racism" as the major factor contributing to the persistent polarization of American society and warned that only a "compassionate, massive, and sustained effort on the part of Government" could avert an impending catastrophe. Ironically, 1968, the date of the Kerner Report, did not usher in a "massive and compassionate Government effort" but marked the termination of the Great Society and the advent of a conservative era.[12] It is not possible to deal with the basic issues afflicting American youth without taking this fundamental truism into account.

The problematic dilemma of two societies defined by color has been compounded by the incorporation into the underclass, by these same criteria, of the greater part of the nation's burgeoning Hispanic population. We have coined a supposedly nonpejorative title for these nonwhite Americans: "minority." The deeply ingrained implicit assumption that "minority" connotes "inferiority" is inferred by our inclination to refer to blacks and Hispanics as minority even when they constitute a majority. Thus, we frequently encounter the doublespeak of a school system, city, association, and so on, composed of a "majority of minorities." The nation's twenty-five largest city school systems, for example, enroll a majority of minorities.[13] Before we are far into the twenty-first century, as many as twelve states could be enrolling a majority of minority children, and the majority of American children entering the first grade might well consist of a majority of minorities.

Obviously the crisis in American education is not caused by the existence of or the rapid growth in the nation's minority population. Yet the pathology associated with the youth crisis is largely concentrated in the cities and communities inhabited disproportionately by Hispanic and black minorities. The elements that constitute this pathology are documented daily in the media: unemployment; homelessness; malnutrition, particularly of the very young; single- or no-parent families; drug and alcohol addiction; high school drop-out rate and low academic performance; violence and crime; teenage nonmarital pregnancy; AIDS; and illiteracy and non-English-language capability. While the latest census data reveal that the life expectancy of Caucasians has increase to 75.4 years, that of the nation's black community has fallen to 69.4 years. Infant mortality data, another important measure of the American dilemma, show that whereas only 8.9 of every 1,000 white babies will die before their first birthday, the number for black infants is twice as high, 18.0. Part of this growing discrepancy is attributable to the escalating homicide incidence and related deaths and to drug-associated afflictions, disproportionately impacting blacks and Hispanics. By 1989 the leading cause of death among black males age fifteen to twenty-four was homicide.

SCHOOLING AND THE PATHOLOGY OF RACISM

The fact that black and Hispanic children consistently score below white and Asiatic children on standardized tests is well documented. What is not well understood is why. The eminent psychologist Dr. Kenneth Clark, who has devoted most of his professional life to questions of minority education and racism, believes that the persistence of racial bias in the nation's schools is a primary factor explaining the correlation of test scores with ethnic origin. As parents of black and Hispanic children are themselves probably victims of discrimination, it is not likely that the home will supply the degree of socialization required to reduce racial stigmatizing effectively. Thus, it is argued, the school must fill this critical role.

It is generally recognized that racial segregation and stereotyping give rise to serious psychological and resultant learning impediments in minority children. The U.S. Supreme Court found that separate but equal schools were inherently unequal on this basis (*Brown* v. *Board of Education*, 1954). Not only have the nation's schools done little to reduce racial stereotyping and racism in American society, but some would argue that they are in fact a major contributor to the American dilemma. Clark believes today, as he did more than thirty years ago, that "education institutions are the chief instrument for the perpetuation of racism."[14] The way in which schools and schooling perpetuate racism are as many as they are stubbornly persistent. The fact that the preponderance of teachers are themselves white, and thus products of a prior generation's hidden curriculum, is certainly an important factor. There is little reason to believe that this situation will change significantly in the foreseeable future. Nationally, black students are twice as apt to be categorized as mentally retarded as are whites.

Whereas 2.3 percent of black youngsters are enrolled as "educable retarded," only 0.87 percent of white children can be found in such classes.

A 1989 report by the Committee for Racial Injustice found that blacks in the nation's public schools were persistently isolated and received an inferior education. This observation was attributed primarily to a pervasive tendency of educators to assume that black youngsters were capable of only relatively low levels of academic attainment.[15]

The teaching profession currently attracts fewer, rather than more, minority college graduates into its ranks. Whereas blacks constituted nearly 11 percent of the total enrollment in the nation's colleges and universities in 1976, their share, despite a substantial increase in the cohort, had fallen to less than 9 percent by 1986. "Twenty nine percent more blacks graduated from high school in 1982 than in 1975, but black enrollment in colleges and universities dropped 11 percent during this period."[16] The escalating use of pre- and in-service teacher tests by state credentialing authorities has also acted to diminish the number of black public school teachers. A recent nineteen-state study reveals that the average passing rate for black candidates was from 15 to 50 percent, in contrast to 71 to 96 percent for white would-be teachers. The recently proposed revamping of the national teacher exams by ETS is in large part a response to cultural bias, which, it is argued, acts to thin the ranks of minority teachers problematically.

Many educators believe that the "hidden curriculum" persistently communicates to minority youngsters and to their teachers that black and Hispanic children are on the average inherently less able and therefore are not capable or expected to perform to "standard," an assumption that becomes a self-fulfilling prophecy. A recent New Orleans public school study found that more than one half of the teachers did not expect their black male students to proceed to higher education. Yet if academic standards are applied as rigorously in the predominantly minority-enrolled inner-city and rural slum schools as they are in the affluent predominantly white suburbs, black and Hispanic youngsters are increasingly flunked out, pushed out, or dropped out. Currently only about one in three black males age eighteen to nineteen is employed. In Chicago, less than half of the ninth graders will in fact graduate from high school, and only half of those who do will read at or above the junior high school level.[17] Nationally more than 40 percent of black seventeen-year-olds are functionally illiterate. Some 38 percent of the nation's urban children who entered high school in 1984 had already dropped out by 1988. In a 1988 study the Detroit Chamber of Commerce concluded that only 7,000 of that city's 20,000 ninth graders will graduate and that only about 500 will be sufficiently educated to qualify for college or university entrance. When one ponders for a moment the long-run national implications of the fact that in cities like Detroit only about 2.1 percent of the youths entering the ninth grade will be eligible to seek a higher education, the catastrophic dimensions of the issue become apparent. The next century's scholars, technicians, teachers, and so on, entered the first grade this year. Clearly the dilemma is as frustratingly complex as are its origins.

Research designed to measure the self-esteem of black youths, replicating a study carried out two decades ago by Clark and associates, concludes that a sense of racial inferiority is as pronounced in today's black youth and children as it was some forty years ago. "What the children are telling us is that they see their color as the basis of self rejection. We have tried to hide the damage that racism does to black children, but the damage is there and will continue as long as racism continues."[18] The study also demonstrated that intensive counseling and education directed specifically to the issue were effective in positively altering one's self-image, thus suggesting that under the right conditions schools and schooling could effectively combat racism. Clark, as well as other authorities, believes that changes and additions to our current educational fare could bring about significant improvement in the self-image of black children. If the pathology of racism results in low self-esteem, leading to poor educational performance and manifesting itself as a major contributor to a national crisis, why have we accomplished so little in more than three decades of post-*Brown* education? Why does the problem appear to be at least as pervasive and unsolvable today as it was a half century ago?

The nexus of racism and schooling is a major factor contributing to the evolution of a permanent underclass in the United States. Effective efforts to confront this phenomenon will require both a heightened sensitivity to the comprehensive dimensions of this national malaise and a corresponding appropriate national public response. But as long as the policy response to this acknowledged national crisis consists of uncoordinated, episodic private sector studies financed and sponsored by foundations and staffed by academics, entreating thousands of relatively autonomous school systems, fifty state governments, parents, and communities to heed and then adopt recommended marginal changes in schools and schooling, there is little likelihood that the self-esteem and thus performance of minority children will be affected positively.

THE IMPORTANCE OF OBJECTIVITY

The question of variable racial performance on standardized tests not only is frustratingly complex but also is extremely sensitive, for it borders on the dangerously contentious terrain of real or perceived racism. Accusations of racism that greeted Daniel Moynihan's seminal work on poverty and the black family in 1963 disinclined a generation of liberal scholars, black and white, from studying and reporting on this critically important issue.[19] However, in recent years it is possible to discern a healthy willingness to confront this sensitive issue. Constructive confrontation and then hopefully progress in resolving this cancerous American dilemma are not likely unless and until all the relevant factors are dealt with openly and impartially. The difficulty of an objective approach to this issue was vividly demonstrated in 1987 when the New York State Board of Regents prepared a drop-out prevention manual for that state's schools. The drop-out problem is overwhelmingly centered in New York's urban predominately minority schools. The manual contained a section that sought to lay out racially specific "learning styles." The authors of the manual

believed that this information would assist educators in tailoring
their style of instruction accordingly and thereby help them cope
with the endemic drop-out problem. The manual reminded New
York's educators that it is important that they take into consideration the fact that Afro-Americans possess "a keen sense of justice
and quick perception of injustice." They are inclined to "view
things in their entirety and not in isolated parts; to approximate
space, number and time, instead of aiming for complete accuracy,
to focus on people and their activities rather than objects."[20] The
fact that black educators were involved in the preparation of this
drop-out prevention manual and that a leading black member of
the sponsoring New York State Board of Regents for Education
was one of its major supporters did not allow the document to
escape scathing denunciation as being itself a racist document.
Regent Adelaide Sanford, an eminent New York educator, referred
to the charges of racism as "a knee jerk response." A black deputy
education commissioner succinctly summed up the dilemma that
educators and others face when they attempt to deal with the
sensitive issue of racial stereotyping:

> What we have here is a lack of willingness to deal with the
> issues on their merit because there is the possibility that there
> may be a racial implication. Well, you can't have it both ways,
> for what we have been doing continues to be unproductive
> for thirty or forty percent of the pupils and a disproportionate
> share of them are black and Hispanic.[21]

The executive director of the state's school board association
advanced the opposing viewpoint: "Caricaturing people by the
color of their skin, or their ethnic origin is racist." He added that
an acceptance of the manual in its original form would be
tantamount to repealing the basic concepts underlying the *Brown*
decision.[22]

While it has been clearly demonstrated that low self-esteem of
minority youngsters contributes significantly to their relatively
poor academic performance and erratic school attendance, it is also

important to note that it also contributes to a sense of personal isolation. Ironically this psychic isolation is compounded by the real isolation brought about by racial segregation. A major 1987 study of school segregation the 1980s reports that there has been virtually no change in the degree of racial segregation of black students over the twelve-year period between 1972 and 1984, with nearly two thirds enrolled in predominantly minority schools.[23] For Hispanics the degree of segregation has increased significantly over this period, from about 57 percent in predominantly minority schools to nearly 71 percent. (A "predominantly minority school" is one in which more than half of the students are minority.)[24] Possibly more indicative of the trend toward resegregation—at least in the North—is the fact that the number of Hispanic students enrolled in schools where 90 percent of the youngsters are minority increased 31 percent in a brief period of four years (1980 to 1984). An examination of the data for one major city is more revealing of the true dimensions of the extraordinary degree of minority isolation that characterizes the nation's inner cities.[25] More than 60 percent of New York City's Hispanic students are enrolled in schools where the minority population constitutes 90 percent or more of the total.[26] The nation's Hispanic population, currently exceeding 20 million, is growing five times as rapidly as the U.S. average. If the current rate of high school graduation of approximately 50 percent persists into the next century, the societal and economic implications of this demographic projection are problematically evident!

A University of Chicago professor of political science who has intensively studied these data recently concluded, "It may well be that the children being socialized and educated in these underclass schools are even more comprehensively isolated from main stream middle-class society than were the black children of the South, whose problems led to the long battle over segregation in Dixie."[27]

There was a time when these problems did not seem so intractable. Segregated schools could be desegregated. Equal educational opportunity and the War on Poverty would, we believed, go a long way to resolve the American dilemma. In retrospect it is evident that our optimism was largely unwarranted. Continued, indeed enhanced, racial segregation and attendant racial isolation, especially in the North, wiped out the few gains made by school desegregation. In city after city the racial balance tipped. Between 1957 and 1977 white enrollment in the nation's urban school systems declined by approximately one-third million students, whereas black and Hispanic enrollment increased by an even greater number.

Increasingly the poverty—the economic and racial isolation and despair—that characterizes the life of children and youth in the inner-city ghettos and rural slums resembles that which we normally associate only with Third World nations. As long as the needs of this most rapidly growing sector of our population are perceived in myopic remedies of improved schools and schooling, divorced from pervasive social, demographic, and economic realities, the American dilemma will proceed to its rendezvous with catastrophe.

It is not possible to consider the magnitude and long-run implications for American society of a youth in crisis without at least briefly touching on the devastation that illicit drugs and the AIDS epidemic are inflicting on the lives of our children and youth. The epidemic of drugs and drug-related AIDS adds to the trauma that is characteristic of the lives of inner-city black and Hispanic youth. Nationally the incidence of AIDS among Hispanics and blacks is twice that of whites. As the nation's relatively well-educated and affluent male gay community mobilizes to confront this deadly disease, the preponderance of inner-city blacks and Hispanics are either ignorant of its means of transmission or so deeply steeped in the despair and hopelessness of their isolated subculture as not to care. It is likely that more AIDS-related deaths are currently attributable to intravenous drug use than to homosexuality. Although they account for 17 percent of our adult population, blacks and Hispanics make up approximately 40 percent of all known AIDS cases.[28] Given the high rate of teenage pregnancy and birth that characterizes the black and Hispanic inner-city population, there is a frightening probability that we will witness a sharp increase in AIDS-infected young mothers and their babies. In

1986, 15 percent of urban area births were those of adolescent mothers. In New York City in 1987 more than 90 percent of the children born with AIDS were either black or Hispanic. AIDS currently is the ninth-ranked cause of death among children one to four years of age and the fifth-ranked for Americans from birth to twenty-four years of age. Even these numbers are deceptive because it is estimated that ten times as many cases go unreported.

Recent studies reveal a close correlation between level of education and frequency of drug addiction. Among heroin addicts entering drug treatment in New York, more than 60 percent are now testing positive for exposure to the AIDS virus.[29]

The extraordinary increase in the incidence of violent crimes in many of the nation's major cities has reached crisis proportions. The current crime wave is clearly associated with the escalating increase in the sale and use of illicit drugs and especially crack. In 1988/89 the exploding incidence of homicide, primarily afflicting minority urban youth, in the nation's major metropolitan areas, tells the story: up more than 55 percent in Washington, 38 percent in Chicago, 35 percent in Detroit, and so on. Washington city policy report that drugs were involved in all but 15 percent of Washington's homicides and that by 1988 nearly two thirds of those arrested tested positive for cocaine.[30]

The preceding has attempted to demonstrate that a nation at risk is less attributable to a general decline in educational productivity than it is to the implications of an emergent permanent underclass composed overwhelmingly of poor urban and rural blacks and Hispanics. The concept of a permanent underclass was developed at length in Ken Auletta's excellent treatment of this subject.[31] This distinction is important because it suggests that a reform strategy based almost exclusively on marginal pedagogical and structural changes in schools and schooling not only is doomed to fail but, more important, tends to obscure the underlying causes of the youth malaise. By consistently posing the wrong questions—questions limited to schools and schooling—we are assured, at best, of the right answers to the wrong questions.

PUBLIC POLICY AND A GENERATION AT RISK

One searches in vain for education reform proposals that would boldly and holistically address the issue of youth at risk—for recommendations that might consider changing the governance structure to create an integrated and coordinated policy process effectively. Fortunately, there is growing evidence that the limitations inherent in a narrowly construed educational reform strategy are beginning to be recognized. For example, by late 1988 the columns of such influential educational writers as Fred Hechinger began to reveal an awareness of and concern about the failure of a decade of educational reform to address the issues of black and Hispanic poverty and alienation. In reviewing what he terms education's "Mixed Report Card," Hechinger writes:

> If you want to file away education's key topics for 1987, consider the topics of "poverty" and "reform." Regrettably poverty was real, while reforms remain largely in blue prints. Yet the two are closely connected: reforms in education were supposed to reduce the damage that poverty does to children. . . . On the whole, 1987 may be notable less for its accomplishments than for harsh facts put before the public: While it is easy to improve suburban education, the schools will continue to fail in their mission unless they improve the education of poor children. . . . The problems of school and society have merged . . . increasing numbers of educators, politicians and citizens [have been forced] to acknowledge that the old ways of running the schools and of teaching in them no longer work. The battle was joined [1987] between those who seek solutions in nostalgia and those who believe that new national problems call for new educational solutions.[32]

Hechinger shares with all of us a more highly developed capacity to identify problems than to come up with innovative solutions. Unfortunately the remedies he proposes, by and large, are but echoes of reforms past. He tells us that "schools can not be improved by orders from the top down."[33] This maxim has been repeated so frequently for so many years that it has assumed the sanctity of the unassailable liturgy that surrounds the educational enterprise, a liturgy that renders it all but impervious to even slightly risqué ideas. In one sense all public schools are governed from the top down, for the state is ultimately the responsible institution for what may or may not occur in the schools. The more fundamental question is what authority should ideally be located at what level in the educational enterprise; but to begin this consideration by promulgating the ancient shibboleth against "authority from the top" (a relative term at best) is to fall into the equally hoary trap of business as usual. Hechinger adds, "Changing the governing bureaucracies matters little, unless real powers are transferred to the school house."[34] It may well be that significantly augmenting the powers at the building level will somehow bring about improvements in the quality of urban life that both Hechinger and the rest of us desire. However, evidence that desired changes follow naturally as a consequence of devolution of authority to the building or to the teacher level is not convincing. In fact, if one is pushed to make a case, the evidence would seem to support the contrary point of view. More and more devolution of power in the face of the frustratingly complex national problems outlined here has about it the neat, unimpeachable simplicity of "return to basics." This is not to say that alterations in the authority structure, involving certain increases in building-level powers, should not be considered under certain circumstances. Indeed, Chapter 5 attempts to sketch some alternative structures that do incorporate enhanced authority at the building level. However, the demonstrated and documented failure of decentralized governance in the nation's major urban school systems, in conjunction with a clear and present national youth and child crisis, suggests that something more imaginative and comprehensive is in order.

Interestingly the recent post-education reform era concern with the more comprehensive issues of a youth in crisis is less a product of foundations, academe, and the educational establishment than of the business community and a number of perceptive state governors.

BUSINESS REDISCOVERS THE SCHOOLS

The enlightened business community is increasingly concerning itself with the broader issues of youth at risk. We say "enlightened" because until recently, with some notable exceptions, American business was inclined to view the plight of American youth and education as if it were a tropical malaise afflicting remote Third World countries. The contributions of the business community to the decade of educational reform, for example, tended to attribute the country's fall from economic grace to the failure of the public schools to guarantee a well-trained, properly motivated, and disciplined labor force. In the late 1980s a number of influential business leaders began to take a more realistic stance, nonetheless one unabashedly in its self-interest. In contrast to the relatively narrow school and schooling focus that characterizes the reform proposals of the education establishment, foundations, and academics, the business community has shown a willingness to grapple with the broader issues of troubled children and youth. In September 1987 the Committee for Economic Development (CED), which counts among is trustees some 200 of the nation's leading business executives, issued a most important document, *Children in Need*, which, in contrast to the education reform reports, fundamentally addresses the interdependent aggregate of problems afflicting millions of poor black and Hispanic children and youth.[35] *Children in Need* does not hesitate to acknowledge the business community's self-interest in alleviating this national dilemma:

> If present trends continue, the scarcity of well educated and well qualified people in the work force will seriously damage this country's competitive position in an increasingly challenging global market place. . . . Our industries will be unable to grow and compete internationally because a growing educational underclass will lack the necessary skills and work habits to function productively on the job.[36]

The business community has studied the changing demographics more astutely than most academics. Increasingly, tomorrow's work force and citizenry, of necessity, will be drawn from the ranks of children currently born and living in poverty. The number of twenty-year-olds available to enter the nation's work force will decline by one fifth by the year 2000. More important is the fact that this declining population will be composed increasingly of minority youth. Unless current trends are arrested and reversed, it is highly unlikely that this increasingly large segment of the nation's population will contribute to either the well-being of the economy or the polity. The problem is national and monumental, for at stake is the very future of the nation. The issue is not at heart educational; in question here is the quality of life in the broadest sense of an emergent America, increasingly black and Hispanic.

Children in Need identifies a number of interrelated approaches that it believes must be put in motion as the cornerstone of an effective public policy. The study recognizes the importance of prenatal and early childhood strategies, which it terms "prevention through early intervention," including programs designed to discourage teenage pregnancy and to provide prenatal and postnatal care for high-risk mothers and family care and developmental care for children, parenting education, child-care facilities, and pre-school programs for all three- and four-year-old disadvantaged children.

The CED study is cognizant of the unique needs of poor black and Hispanic children and youth and boldly proposes a major restructuring of education. The report calls for including support systems such as health services and psychological, career, and family counseling as integral components of the school setting. The bold and imaginative ideas that characterize the CED's proposals concerning early childhood and child-care services are conspicuously absent when the report addresses reforming public education. Its recommendations in this area do not differ markedly from the orthodoxy: better school management, including more shared decision making involving teachers; more committed and more minority teachers; smaller schools and smaller classes; improved educational technology; more emphasis on extracurricular activities, and so on.

The CED concludes its Executive Summary with a cautionary note that appears somewhat inconsistent with its bold analysis and assessment of children in need: "We caution the states to resist the temptation to supplant local authority. Local school districts and individual schools should be provided with enough discretionary power so that programs are kept small in scale, remain manageable and flexible, and are able to be individualized."[37] While the CED is prepared to confront the holistic dimensions of the nation's risk, it is not prepared to contemplate even minimal structural changes in the nation's system of public education that conceivably might provide a more effective policy process. Still unaddressed is the question of how the CED can be assured that some 16,000 school boards, a comparable number of other local authorities, and fifty state governments will hear its pleas and as a consequence voluntarily institute its recommendations. If history is a worthy guide, and particularly the record of decentralized urban educational governance, there is little reason to believe that simply pointing the direction, or even holding out the availability of matching state or federal dollars, will in some miraculous fashion institute the programs that the CED wisely proposes.

A persistent theme in Americana is that most successful institutions borrow from or emulate business. There may be some truth to this observation. With respect to education it has been observed that one of the problems afflicting the schools is that whereas they successfully mimicked earlier twentieth-century industrial organization, the schools have failed to keep up with management changes that characterize the business "renaissance." Whereas business has embraced decentralization, worker involvement, and consultation, education, it is suggested, persists in heavy-handed dysfunctional bureaucratic management policies. What works for business ought to work for education. With this in mind a number of major corporations, properly concerned about the availability of a highly skilled, technically able work force for the twenty-first century, have decided to demonstrate the effectiveness of their techniques by directly operating inner-city schools. For example, sixteen major corporations have banded together and opened on Chicago's poor west side what they promise to be but the first of many "model" urban schools: "We intend to show the public school system how a city school should be managed."[38] Some $2 million have been raised to manage a school donated to the corporate group by the Catholic dioceses to enroll about 150 elementary students. The sum is obviously much greater than that anticipated by the average Chicago public school. But then the corporate model will be open year-round and from early morning to late in the day. Governance of this corporately funded inner-city school is not to be turned over to the community. The board is to be composed of five representatives from their corporate sponsors, three local educators, and three people from the community. The school will incorporate a wide range of child services other than education and will attempt to bring about active parental partici-pation, in part by arranging for the teachers to visit the parents in their homes. The underlying assumption, once again, is that the fundamental problem is basically one of school and schooling. Were this indeed the case, there would be much to be said for this well-meaning and hopefully successful experiment.

Education and related demographic data, and particularly the excellent analysis provided by Harold Hodgkinson of the Institute for Educational Leadership, increasingly are studied by a business community concerned as to where it will find the high-quality work force required for the twenty-first century. Over the next decade approximately 20 million new workers will join the nation's labor force. More important, however, is that all but about 7 percent of this number will be composed of minorities, immi-grants, and women. American business is increasingly aware that unless radical changes significantly increase the level and quality of education achieved by minority and immigrant youth, the United States is in danger of becoming a second-rate economic power. Pepsi-Cola laid out its rationale for a $2 million program to improve education in two urban high schools: "The uneducated or the undereducated are simply not capable of operating the systems and machinery of any increasingly advanced high technology society."[39]

Major corporations are increasingly involving themselves directly in the acknowledged youth and child crisis. General Electric, for example, is operating a program for poor minority students in the South that involves intensive after-school tutoring. Hopefully this trend will persist and grow. In 1987 American corporations provided the nation's colleges and universities with about $1.8 billion. Precollege-level contributions, though growing, amounted to less than $200 million.

Recent years have seen a marked increase in the provision of private support for public education. In part this tendency is due to state- and court-inspired "equalization" policies that have sought to diminish per pupil expenditure differentials between rich and poor school systems. Relatively affluent communities have responded by resorting to private donations from parents and other members of the community for school programs that ordinarily would be funded with tax dollars. Extracurricular program expenses increasingly are supported in this fashion. More important is the propensity to purchase in this manner otherwise unavailable expensive laboratory and computer equipment. This trend in conjunction with an uncoordinated enhanced role by the business community raises serious questions of equity. It is increasingly evident that relatively successful efforts to further equal educational opportunity for all children—rich and poor, black and white—are being circumvented by the relative ease and willingness of affluent communities to make substantial private funding available to their public schools. To the extent to which equal educational opportunity for all American children is a vital national interest, a policy process that furthers the subsidy of already advantaged youngsters is contrary to that interest.

GOVERNORS REDISCOVER THE SCHOOLS

An increasing awareness on the part of the business community and the nation's governors of the centrality of the condition of minority children and youth to the nation's risk, even if not accompanied by a comparable appreciation of the necessity to reexamine the adequacy of the existent policy process, is encouraging.

In 1988 New York's governor Mario Cuomo proclaimed 1989 to be the beginning of "The Decade of the Child."[40] Along with a number of other farsighted governors, Cuomo has launched a number of legislative proposals that reflect a growing awareness that the deteriorating condition of inner-city, predominantly minority children and youth is a matter vital to the welfare of the state and the nation. While the governor's 1988 budget message did not call for significant increases in expenditure for traditional areas of public education, it did request substantial new monies for child- and youth-related services. It included, for example, a request for some $25 million for a pilot prekindergarten program, but more important, it was accompanied by the governor-stated intent of making prekindergarten services available for all New York four-year-olds by 1992.[41] Governor Cuomo's words are indicative of an increasingly pragmatic approach to this long-neglected problem: "Efforts on the behalf of families and children are no longer just a matter of self-interest. . . . They are a matter of economic survival in the 21st century."[42]

In neighboring New Jersey, Governor Kean displayed a similar awareness. In January 1988 he announced a new state program designed to bring a wide variety of services to disadvantaged youth in an effort to deal comprehensively with what is increasingly perceived to be much more than an educational issue:

A six million dollar program will offer counseling, health services, and employment referrals, to address drug and alcohol abuse problems, high suicide rates, mental illness, and emotional problems and teen age pregnancy, that makes learning difficult and contributes to decisions by 20,000 students each year to drop out.[43]

New Jersey's commissioner of Human Services, charged with

responsibility for much of the new program, concluded that "the time has come to bring human services and education together. . . . The boundaries don't work anymore. They need us and we need them."[44] Comparable programs have been initiated in many other states. However, there is little coordination other than a degree of program replication. Proceedings of recent Governors Conferences reveal a sophisticated awareness of both the holistic dimensions and the national gravity of the crisis afflicting poor, predominantly minority youth. However, it is not possible to expect that a coherent national policy will somehow evolve as a product of the efforts of many but not all state governors. It is only recently that a number of the nation's governors, often prodded by the business community, have detected political mileage in education, child, and youth concerns. This momentary political mileage is critically reliant on a continued growth in revenues, which in turn is highly dependent on the state of the economy. By 1989 New York's Governor Cuomo and New Jersey's Governor Kean were talking less about expanding services for poor minority children and youth and more about where and how to cut services in order to cope with drastic downturns in revenue expectations.

Chapter 5 critically examines a number of traditional reform strategies that are frequently proposed to bring about the desired changes in education and related child and youth services. Chapter 5 concludes by suggesting some possibly more appropriate, albeit more controversial, policy approaches to a nation at risk.

NOTES

1. See Lauren Resnick, "The Presidential Address: Learning in School and Out," *Educational Researcher* 16:9 (December 1987):13–20.

2. Leonard Bruder, "Decentralization of Schools Provides Painful Lessons," *New York Times*, 11 December 1988, IV:6.

3. Quoted in Neil A. Lewis, "School Boards Found Failing to Meet Goals," *New York Times*, 5 December 1988, II:1.

4. John Chubb, "To Revive Schools, Dump Bureaucrats," *New York Times*, 9 December 1988, I:35.

5. Hugh Davis Graham, *The Uncertain Triumph: Federal Education Policy in the Kennedy and Johnson Years* (Chapel Hill: University of North Carolina Press, 1984), 144.

6. Ibid., 145–46.

7. Ibid., 196.

8. Roberto Suro, "John Paul Assails Economic Plight of Blacks in U.S.," *New York Times*, 13 September 1987, I:1.

9. William Julius Wilson, *The Inner City and Public Policy* (Chicago: University of Chicago Press, 1987), 7.

10. Ibid., 7.

11. Gunnar Myrdal, *An American Dilemma* (New York: Harper & Row, 1969).

12. Richard Bernstein, "20 Years after the Kerner Report: Three Societies, All Separate," *New York Times*, 29 February 1988, I:8.

13. Harold Hodgkinson, *All One System: Demographics of Education, Kindergarten through Graduate School* (Washington, D.C.: Institute for Educational Leadership, 1985), 16.

14. Kenneth Clark, quoted in Thomas Morgan, "U.S. Schools Are Said to Fail in Reducing Bias," *New York Times*, 3 May 1987, I:55.

15. Julie Johnson, "Schools Faulted on Educating Blacks," *New York Times*, 24 May 1989, II:8.

16. Hodgkinson, *All One System*, 16.

17. Wilson, *The Inner City and Public Policy*, 56.

18. Kenneth Clark, quoted in Daniel Goleman, "Black Child's Self-View Is Still Low, Study Finds," *New York Times*, 31 August 1987, I:13.

19. Daniel Patrick Moynihan and Nathan Glazer, *Beyond the Melting Pot: The Negroes, Puerto Ricans, Jews, Italians, and Irish of New York City* (Cambridge: MIT Press, 1963).

20. Sam Roberts, "The Race Factor: Do Educators See Differences?" *New York Times*, 16 November 1987, II:1.

21. Irving Hamer, Jr., quoted in Roberts, "The Race Factor," II:1.

22. Ibid.

23. From the report "School Segregation in the 1980s" by the University of Chicago, cited in Edward Fiske, "Hispanic Pupils' Plight Cited in Study," *New York Times*, 26 July 1987, I:24.

24. Ibid.

25. Ibid.

26. Ibid.

27. Professor Gary Orfield, quoted in ibid., I:24.

28. William E. Schmidt, "High AIDS Rate Spurring Efforts for Minorities," *New York Times*, 2 August 1987, I:1.

29. Dr. Benny Primm of the Addiction Research and Treatment Corporation, quoted in Peter Kerr, "Rich vs. Poor: Drug Patterns Are Diverging," *New York Times*, 30 August 1987, I:28.

30. Richard L. Berke, "Capitol Offers a Ripe Market to Drug Dealers," *New York Times*, 28 March 1989, I:16.

31. The dimensions and implications of a permanent underclass was powerfully spelled out by Ken Auletta in *The Underclass* (New York: Random House, 1982).

32. Fred M. Hechinger, "87's Mixed Report Card," *New York Times*, 29 December 1987, III:11.

33. Ibid.

34. Ibid.

35. Committee for Economic Development, Research and Policy Committee, *Children in Need: Investment Strategies for the Educationally Disadvantaged* (New York: Committee for Economic Development, 1987).

36. Ibid., 5.

37. Ibid., 18.

38. Dirk Johnson, "Companies Create 'Model School' for Urban Poor," *New York Times*, 26 October 1988, II:10.

39. Doron P. Levin, "$2 Million Awards Program Aims to Cut School Dropouts," *New York Times*, 18 May 1989, I:18.

40. New York Governor Mario Cuomo, "State of the State Address," *New York Times*, 7 January 1988, I:1.

41. Mario Cuomo, "Excerpts from Governor's Budget Message

to the Legislature: Cuomo Asks Increases for Education and Housing," *New York Times*, 14 January 1988, II:5.

42. Ibid.

43. Governor of New Jersey Thomas Kean, quoted by Joseph F. Sullivan, "Program to Aid Troubled Youths: Jersey Schools Will Offer Counseling on Drug Abuse and Family Problems," *New York Times*, 10 January 1988, I:27.

44. New Jersey Commission of Human Services, quoted in ibid., I:27.

5

Reform Strategies and Policies

The many proposals that have come to characterize the current dialogue on education reform vary from some that would return to the supposed rigors and excellence of yesteryear, most that would essentially raise the standards that define existing pedagogies and the teaching profession, to a few that go so far as to propose that the public school system be abolished. In this chapter this range of alternatives is explored to demonstrate the important relationship between the prevailing governance philosophy, outlined above, and the nature of the remedies that are currently being implemented or considered for implementation.

ASSESSMENT OF CONVENTIONAL REFORM POLICIES AND STRATEGIES

As noted briefly in Chapter 1, the spate of reports that dominated the discourse on educational reform during the early years of this decade were characterized more by their monotonous similarity than by bold originality. Most of the recommendations concerned the teaching profession. Proposals to increase teacher salaries to attract potentially superior candidates into the profession were an integral part of nearly all the reform reports. Obviously this concern with teacher quality is indicative of the prevailing view that the crisis in education can be attributed, in important part, to the dearth of well-qualified effective and dedicated classroom teachers. This focus on instructional quality is also responsible for the host of reform proposals that would entice and reward "good," and discourage and penalize "bad," teachers and would-be teachers. Most of the proposals advanced to achieve this end have been around for many years. Merit pay, for example, which is commonplace in higher education, until recent years was successfully blocked by the determined opposition of teacher unions.

The public's concern over declining student performance, ignited by the media's documentation and by the spate of well-publicized commission reports, empowered governors and legislators in many (but not all) states to generate substantial new revenues devoted to funding the bewildering array of strategies designed to improve the teaching profession. There is a danger, however, that failure of the many expensive, frequently untested teacher improvement strategies to achieve their intended purposes will contribute to a decline in public support for education. It is important to recall that less than one third of the nation's voters have children in the public schools. During times of relative economic plenty and in an era that is momentarily characterized by a willingness to support education, it is politically feasible to secure the increased revenues necessary to fund the reforms. But once reform enthusiasm wanes, once American industry, for whatever reason, perceives a labor surplus, once the economy turns down, as has already occurred in a number of states, there is a real likelihood that political steam will exit the education reform movement.

By the turn of the century, more than one third of the children in our public, tax-supported elementary and secondary schools will be black or Hispanic. Despite recent evidence that the nation's minority citizens are beginning to flex their political muscle, it is not likely that they will soon exercise influence proportionate to their numbers. Nor is it likely that they will soon aggregate sufficient voting power to counter that of the dominant majority, most of whom do not have children in public schools and who are less and less inclined to support taxation to pay for the education of other people's children. This eventuality is all the more likely if the myriad of expensive, locally episodic, often haphazardly installed reform efforts do not show evidence of stemming the educational decline. If costly expanding enrollment, especially of minority children, is accompanied by media-publicized failure of the expensive reform programs, public and political support can be expected to decline even further.

Between 1986 and 1990 the public school population will have increased by more than 2 million children. Even if everything else remains unchanged, this fact alone will require an extraordinary increase in annual expenditures for education. The costs of an array of expensive programs designed to improve teacher quality with a view to significantly improving the performance of students will have to be funded, of necessity, over and above what is dictated by an expanding school population. The long-range implications of such fiscal realities to the future of the educational reform movement are placed in stark perspective when it is noted that the implementation of only those reform proposals recommended by the National Commission on Excellence would entail a 20 percent per pupil increase in educational expenditure.[1] The recommendation of the Carnegie Forum on Education and the Economy, summarized earlier, would require additional revenues of approximately $48 billion over a ten-year period.[2]

Once the political mileage in education runs out, it is unlikely that governors and would-be governors will campaign on platforms advocating massive increases in educational expenditure. In most states the local property tax remains the mainstay supporting the nation's schools. Property taxpayers are disproportionately representative of the population without children in the public schools. Therefore, it is unrealistic to anticipate from a predominantly white middle-class, middle-aged population with few, if any, of their own children in the public schools substantial political support in favor of increased levels of taxation to support additional educational expenditures.

The vagaries and variations in state and local resources, and associated political inclinations, will continue to limit educational expenditure absolutely as well as to guarantee a continued wide discrepancy in per pupil support between and within the fifty states and 16,000 school districts. An educational policy process consisting of the sum of the parts of the policies of fifty states and 16,000 schools districts, therefore, can hardly be expected to equitably address the acknowledged national crisis in education.

LIMITATIONS OF TEACHER REFORM STRATEGIES

Of comparable importance to the economic and political variables noted above is the possibility that the spate of teacher improvement reforms, even if funded and implemented, will not significantly affect the quality of education. For example, the few data that exist suggest that teachers are not primarily motivated by monetary rewards. One of the few studies of this relationship concluded that money "was a disincentive for teacher change."[3] The relationship of teacher retention to salary does not seem to support the argument that increasing monetary rewards will positively incline teachers to remain in the profession. North Dakota teachers, for example, have the second highest rate of retention (84.9 percent) but are tenth from the bottom in terms of salary.[4] "Career ladders," another conventional alternative also initially opposed by the teacher unions, have been instituted in the schools in nearly half of the states. A career ladder strategy is based on the assumption that an incentive pay plan rewarding teachers and administrators for extraordinary service or excellence will lead to improved student performance as well as incline the best faculty to remain in the profession. Most career ladder plans require that a beginning teacher serve a two- or three-year internship under the tutelage of a "mentor" before proceeding to the next rung on the career ladder. In time, and assuming adequate performance, the professional teacher, with appropriate salary increases, can be promoted to "lead teacher," and so on. Susan Rosenholtz, who has studied the relationship of teacher performance as affected by a number of reform strategies, tells us that available research indicates that competition engendered by policies such as differential pay and career ladders tends "to close rather than open communication and sharing among those who work together, to bias comprehension of differing view points, and to destroying trust among group members. . . . In fact, competitive conditions may lead people to deliberately frustrate the attempts of others to succeed."[5] Furthermore, it is not likely that rewards to which one is entitled only after a lengthy tenure will effectively incline the new and the best teachers to stay the course.

Sabbaticals, forgivable tuition loans, and improved working conditions such as fewer and smaller classes and a reduction in red tape and other noninstructional duties are also a part of the reform agenda in most states. Despite the fact that these strategies have been around for decades, no reliable data exist demonstrating their effectiveness measured by either "improvement" in teacher quality or in student performance. The wholesale introduction of such reform strategies, with but little other than common sense evidence that they can achieve their intended purposes, unfortunately can contribute to public disillusionment and thereby to the curtailment of the reform efforts.

RESTRUCTURING OF SCHOOLS

The second cluster of conventional reform strategies is concerned less with teachers than with restructuring the schools. "Restructuring of schools" is not precisely defined. It is employed generally to describe any reform proposal that gives the appearance of being something more profound than a strategy of marginal improvement.

To some school restructuring means the introduction of more personalized pedagogical techniques, to others it infers expanded parental choice as to the school their children attend, and to many pundits it entails a devolution of authority over curriculum, employment, and budget to the school building level. Obviously such strategies require a bit more audacity, for many of the changes proposed are considerably more fundamental than merely tinkering with teacher working conditions and reward structures. Involved are strategies that would change the conventional instructional process; revise teaching methods; place more emphasis on critical thinking and less on rote learning; encourage greater and more imaginative use of instructional technology, peer tutoring, community-based experiential education, and a variety of alternative programs; create magnet schools; bring about changes in the length of the school day and school year; alter after-school and summer classes; devise new kinds of reward systems for children; and so on. The list is essentially endless, and most of these "bold" alternative strategies have been around for many years.

The educational reform landscape is strewn with the debris of thousands of experimental, pilot model programs that seemed to some, in one brief moment, to promise delivery of the elusive miracle and to possess the potential of universal applicability and thus national acceptance. Indeed, many of these isolated uncoordinated experiments did achieve extraordinary—but with few exceptions, momentary—success. Over the long haul such programs rarely outlive the involvement and commitment of their enthusiastic initiators and proponents or their initial pilot funding. There simply is no evidence that an array of sporadic, unrelated reform programs, funded in a variety of complex ways, will ever evolve a national educational policy. A few examples of the more imaginative school restructuring efforts are presented to demonstrate their extraordinary variety but, unfortunately, their frailty as well.

The Cleveland school system, in cooperation with a group of civic leaders, recently announced a grandiose plan to award scholarship monies to its 30,000 seventh to twelfth graders. The scheme would credit a student's college escrow account with funds, the amount depending on his or her letter grades in certain courses. The object of this unusual venture is to curb that city's 50 percent drop-out rate. The program, estimated to cost $3 million a year, will look to the private sector, foundations, corporations, and individuals for its funding. There is little evidence that such a delayed reward structure will motivate marginal students to stay in school. Relevant research suggests that factors other than availability or nonavailability of college tuition support correlate with a propensity to drop out or to stay in school. Those youngsters that do build up a substantial tuition escrow fund are most likely to be the same students that would qualify for existing student-aid packages. Furthermore, the haphazard funding plan for this program all but guarantees that it will have a brief life; if so, its failure would be all the more unfortunate for having raised expectations that likely will not be met.

In 1988 New York's Governor Cuomo proposed a somewhat similar scheme for that state's impoverished high school graduates. "Liberty Scholarships" would be made available to students whose family's income was less than 1.3 times the poverty level. This well-intended program suffers from the same limitations as those noted above. There are few data showing a relationship between the proposed means and the anticipated ends. The sporadic, often haphazard, initiation of such strategies, even if and when they are effective, from a national point of view, impact but a tiny fraction of the country's children and youth, while at the same time further aggravating existing inequalities in per pupil opportunity and support.

As long as the educational policy process remains chaotic and fragmented, there is little likelihood that a relatively uniform and more equalitarian national educational program will evolve. And as long as the process consists essentially of a nonpublic network of educational professionals, academics, foundations, and related institutions, it is likely that the proposed reform strategies will be conservative, limited primarily to orthodox tactics to improve teacher quality and school restructuring. Such reforms, by and large, will be pertinent to schools, rather than to children, and to schools attended by middle-class, predominantly white pupils.

FREEDOM OF CHOICE—
THE ULTIMATE DECENTRALIZATION

The provision of greater choice for parents as to which schools their children attend is also an increasingly attractive reform strategy, one possessed of a long lineage. The advocates of vouchers, for example, argue that because the public schools are encumbered with tenure statutes, collective bargaining, and a stifling bureaucracy, they are beyond salvation unless they are required to compete for students on a roughly equal basis with the private sector. The provision of vouchers, or the granting of tax credits for private school tuition, it is argued, would improve the public schools by requiring that they make the changes necessary to enable them to compete with the private sector. Ironically, Myron Liberman, a leading scholarly proponent of vouchers and private schools as a viable solution to the education crisis, also shares this writer's view that a fundamental change in the governance structure is one viable road to reform. In his recent book, which makes a cogent case for vouchers, he concludes that "the process of education will improve only in response to (a) changes in its governance structure, that is, the way education is organized, financed, and controlled; and/or (b) the expansion of non-public education."[6] Predictably Liberman rejects his first but embraces his second alternative.

Over the past two decades the debate over vouchers and such related measures as tuition tax credits has become a perennial and divisive issue in the politics of education. A combination of support from the Catholic church and from ideological conservatives has exerted a constant pressure on the political process; for a quarter century legislation has been regularly introduced at both state and federal levels to legitimize vouchers and tuition tax credits. It is persuasively argued that the existing "public school monopoly" locks students into attending specific schools solely because of where they happen to reside, thus, in effect, contributing to racial and class segregation. A wider range of choice, subsidized for the poor by vouchers and tax credits, it is contended, would allow

parents to choose their preferred school, with the result
dents and their families would seek out schools consistent w..
their particular interests, rather than being required to attend the
same school as children living in what are often residentially
segregated neighborhoods.

The antivoucher argument contends that private schools subsidized by vouchers and/or tuition tax credits would incline the
highly motivated, brighter, and most likely middle-class students
to flee the public schools, with the result that they would be left
with only those children who, for whatever reason, are unable to
move or gain admission into private schools. The likely negative
impact that a predominantly private school system would have on
the historic relationship of public schooling to the vital traditions
that constitute the nation's political and cultural heritage is also
advanced by the opponents of vouchers and tax credits. A significant weakening of the public school system resulting from a
substantial voucher policy, it is argued, would inevitably and
dangerously erode support for the nation's fundamental values.

A number of states have introduced various forms of tuition tax
credit. Minnesota, for example, allows state income tax deductions
for tuition paid to private and parochial schools. The little evidence
that exists suggests that few families decide for or against sending
their children to private schools because of the availability of
tuition tax credits. To the extent to which this observation is correct
the net effect of tuition tax credits is to subsidize predominantly
middle-class families, who would have sent their children to
private schools in any case.

The opponents of vouchers remind us that it is not only the
individual student and his or her family that have a vested interest
in the education of the nation's children. The public school system
exists in important part to provide, or at least to attempt to provide,
a "common" experience, one that will provide future citizens with
shared values and knowledge requisite to the maintenance of the
society and polity. Private schools competing with one another for
students would be tempted to ignore or to shortcut their public
responsibilities in order to lower costs, to provide attractive non-

public programs, or to emphasize their particular values and beliefs. This writer recalls a protracted dispute with an experimental
avant-garde school in New Jersey that stubbornly opposed a state
requirement that students be taught American history, for it was
deemed to be counter to its philosophy of "freedom of choice."

The opponents of public support for private schools are also
inclined to remind voucher proponents, of the left and the right,
that a suspiciously large federal bureaucracy would be required to
monitor such an alternative policy. More than a few influential
leaders of the private school sector, as well as political conservatives, have expressed considerable concern that the likely controls
implicit in federal monitoring and ensuing regulation may be too
high a price to pay for Uncle Sam's largess.

The Reagan administration, consistent with its campaign
pledges, sought, on a number of occasions, to move legislation to
permit the granting of vouchers to those parents choosing to send
their children to private schools. Attempts by the Reagan administration in 1983 and again in 1985 to secure passage of a comprehensive general voucher system were vehemently opposed by
teacher unions and the educational establishment. The proposed
legislation died in committee. More recently, Department of Education officials, in a compromise maneuver, proposed legislation
that would provide vouchers to reimburse private schools for the
costs of remedial education for children from poor families in those
instances in which the appropriate public school did not provide
such services. The funds to finance this proposed administration
voucher program were to be taken from the appropriation for Title
I of the Elementary and Secondary Education Act—this, despite
the fact that this act currently funds considerably less than half of
the potentially eligible youngsters.

Voucher proposals have persisted as a viable and attractive
policy alternative for nearly a half century despite the overwhelming opposition of the public school community and the educational
establishment. The persistence of this alternative structure is in part
attributable to the fact that support for private education is forthcoming from both the conservative Right and the liberal Left. A

number of leading liberals support vouchers for the same reasons that they categorically oppose a significant governance role for public institutions in education. Vouchers, and related strategies such as tuition tax credits, have become highly politicized, in part because of their significance to the nation's parochial and religious schools. Because the issue is so volatile, it is in many respects a stalking horse for noneducational controversies. Unfortunately the debate rarely takes into account the more comprehensive concerns of troubled urban and predominantly minority children and youth. However, some private school advocates of federal support in the form of vouchers maintain that although they are prepared to enroll increasing numbers of minority youngsters, their capacity to subsidize the education of urban minority youth privately is inadequate to the demands already being put upon them, and to do so would require federal support. Former Secretary of Education William Bennett suggested that Catholic schools open their doors even wider to impoverished students, hinting that this would somehow elicit political support for federal funding.

Freedom of choice as an alternative to the orthodoxy of assigned school of attendance has grown in popularity in recent years. Nearly half of the states have or plan legislation authorizing freedom of choice. Although the variety of freedom of choice proposals and policies that surfaced in the late 1980s differ considerably, they tend to permit parents to send their children to a school of their choice within a given jurisdiction, with equivalent public funds following the child. The proponents of freedom of choice argue that it enables parents to place their children in schools particularly suited to their needs and talents. It is also suggested that freedom of choice would reward the excellent schools and either improve poor schools or lead to their demise. Efforts of school administrators to attract students would, it is argued, lead to innovative programs and to healthy competition. In 1989 the Minnesota legislature passed legislation permitting parents to enroll their children in schools outside their district of residence. The Boston school system has embarked on a similar policy citywide. The Bush administration has strongly endorsed freedom of choice programs and went so far as to sponsor a White House workshop on this alternative in 1989.

As with other trends promoting decentralization and an enhanced parental role, freedom of choice supporters are to be found on both the left and the right of the political spectrum. Conservatives argue that competition between public schools is inherently healthy. Liberals, and especially those from academe, see freedom of choice as consistent with a diminished role for government, and as a way to provide an opportunity for disadvantaged youngsters to attend superior suburban schools.

In conjunction with decentralization of decision making over personnel, curriculum, and finance to the community, teachers and building levels, freedom of choice will act to remove the governance of education from the public policy process further. Conceivably, individual schools, each governed by its unique council of teachers, parents, and community, will be in a position to craft a curriculum and educational staff with the intent of attracting more and more of the kind of students that it deems desirable. Students not fortunate enough to have parents, or at least parents that are sufficiently interested in and motivated to seek out "the best" school will end up disproportionately in the "poorer" schools. The net effect is likely to be further segregation and isolation.

To the extent to which decentralization tends toward governance similar to that of private schools, there is a possibility that some schools will tailor their programs less to educational excellence than to highly publicized specialized programs designed to attract the public funding following the student. One might even expect to see advertisements in papers, on television, and on subways and buses enticing students to attend a given school with the promise of jobs and higher education opportunities. It is also likely that school administrators, in order to keep their best students from transferring, will skew programs away from poor students with the greatest needs, and toward their brightest youngsters. The sordid history of many, but certainly not all, proprietary trade schools should provide a useful object lesson. One might argue that because they are public, the freedom of choice schools would be immune to such misrepresentation and profit seeking. However, decentralizing authority to the community/school level, given past experience with this approach, could provide ample opportunity to avoid public accountability and to operate the schools less in the interests of the education of children and youth than in the interests of personal gain.

Also lost in the trend toward decentralized freedom of choice schools is the fundamental American idea of the "common school." If one is free to choose any school, and if school governance is decentralized to the point where the purposes, curriculum, and philosophy of the schools are set idiosyncratically, it is conceivable that the nation's public common school system will degenerate into highly particularized institutions or associations of institutions oriented toward specific ethnic, religious, ideological, or political tenets, with obvious implications for the nation.

David Kearns, Xerox chief executive officer (CEO), has emerged as a leading and articulate spokesperson for the business community as it seeks increasingly to influence the future of public education in the United States. He suggests that the competitive process, characteristic of American business, provides a most relevant model for public education, which, in his view, suffers the consequences of monopoly control over the school enterprise. The questionable image of business in contemporary America, with respect to either productivity or ethics, might lead some to question the universal applicability of this model. Kearns recommends that parents be permitted to send their children to a school of their choice. This, he concludes, would lead to the emergence of tailored magnet schools and to the proper demise of unpopular, unsuccessful schools. Teachers and administrators would design their own distinctive institutions, set the curriculum, and select the textbooks. Just how the public interest in the education of its children and youth would be ensured by such an approach is unclear. One wonders how Kearns and his colleagues in the business community would react to a school, or to an association of schools, that adopted a radically socialistic, anticapitalistic, or even anti-American educational philosophy, replete with relevant textbooks and curricula.

The involvement of the business community in the national educational/youth crisis, and especially the interest and commitment of persons such as Kearns, is critical to the nation's future. From the point of view of this writer, however, it would be desirable if more thought were given to the national dimensions of the crisis and the relationship of such dimensions to desperately needed structural reform.

NATIONAL TESTS AND A NATIONAL CURRICULUM

Recent efforts to nationalize teacher preparation and certification programs and to expand considerably the national student testing program reflect a growing realization that continued anarchy in this vital area seriously obstructs meaningful and equitable reform in public education. Not surprisingly, the debate over the relative merits of competing policies to bring about even a minimum of national uniformity has stirred the same hornet's nest as those noted above. The proponents of local control, and those who are distrustful of a significant policy role for the federal government, argue, for example, that uniform standardized tests are but a precursor to a uniform national curriculum, this despite evidence that the American public overwhelmingly supports the idea of a national curriculum.

Rarely are the arguments for or against a minimal national curriculum rationally developed or advanced. To argue against this reform strategy effectively, it is sufficient to raise the possibility that a national curriculum "might" evolve in the wake of a comprehensive national testing program. Ernest Boyer, president of the Carnegie Foundation for the Advancement of Teaching, provided some credence to this point of view when he remarked, "Testing is a way to short circuit the discussion of what we want our schools to teach. . . . We can agree more on our tests than on our goals."[7]

Proposals to expand the federal government–sponsored standardized testing program (National Assessment of Educational Progress) have been sporadically advanced in Congress for more than two decades. The current proposed legislation would broaden the program to cover additional subject areas and more students, as well as permit a state-by-state comparison of test scores, a revelation that until recently was opposed by the great majority of governors and state educational officials. Surprisingly, the proposed legislation, although studiously avoiding a preponderant role for the federal government, does contain provisions that would diminish the dominance of the private sector and enhance the relative responsibilities of the federal government. After having been initially administered and managed by the ECS, the current national testing program was subsequently entrusted to the ETS, advised by panels of educators and other professionals. The proposed changes would transfer authority to a national assessment governing board, whose members would be appointed by the U.S. Secretary of Education from a list drawn up by the board. The secretary would have considerable authority to determine the content of at least some of the proposed national tests. Not surprisingly, this enhanced role for the federal government is viewed with apprehension by many in the educational establishment. More power in Washington, it is feared, not only would escalate what is perceived by many to be a dangerous trend toward a uniform national curriculum but would also act to entrench a public policy process that would inevitably determine what all American children should be expected to know and to do as a consequence of their education, regardless of where and under whose apparent authority it occurs.

POWER TO THE TEACHERS

A persistent theme in the reform dialogue attributes much of education's problems to the powerlessness of teachers. Despite considerable evidence that decentralization of decision making to the community and school level has done little to improve student outcomes and indeed may be responsible for much of the chaos that characterizes education in many of the nation's largest cities, the major teacher unions as well as a number of academic writers and influential academics advocate further decentralization of the educational policy process. This growing demand for enhanced authority at the building level and for a significantly expanded policy role for teachers is of such a magnitude and of such potential importance that it is treated in some detail below.

An astute policy historian might contend that episodic efforts to transfer authority over major social programs from relatively centralized public institutions to a frequently ill-defined people or community occur approximately every thirty years or so in the United States. Centralization atrophies; bureaucracy becomes bloated, insensitive, and irresponsible. Reform movements respond by dismantling the bureaucracy and by "redecentralizing." Idealistically perceived community institutions, in turn, are captured by special interests and essentially become but agencies for patronage and contract allocation. The media, the political institutions, and the public respond by significantly narrowing the authority and prerogatives of the local community. Delegated responsibility is returned to a supposedly more efficient, less corrupt, and relatively centralized agency of government; and then the cycle repeats itself.

The current era of educational reform is characterized by a growing awareness of the necessity to evolve comprehensive nationally applicable policy to socialize and educate all the nation's youth, regardless of where they live or what their socioeconomic levels are. However, the growing awareness is accompanied by a contrary propensity. The educational establishment increasingly advocates the allocation of authority for public education, and responsibility for the socialization of the nation's children and youth, to a diffuse and scattered array of millions of individual school building administrators, teachers, and parents. This dichotomous policy is partly a product of the recommendations contained in the many reform reports for nearly every major set of recommendations includes proposals to empower teachers and building-level administrators and to shrink state and local regulations and authority.

Before analyzing the variety of specific programs that have surfaced in response to these recommendations, it is necessary to examine briefly the reasons why teacher prerogatives and authority have steadily eroded over the past three decades.

THE STATUS OF THE TEACHING PROFESSION

Over the past two decades the eroding quality of the teaching profession, as determined by a variety of tests measuring the academic performance of teachers and would-be teachers, has been voluminously studied and documented. One major study of the teaching occupation concluded, "It is clear that low-scoring, whether black or white, are disproportionately represented by the population recruited to teaching, those who actually teach, and those who remain in teaching. . . . Fully 60% of the white teachers committed to teaching at age thirty score below 60% of all college graduates."[8] The data suggest that the best-qualified teachers are most likely to leave the profession, with the result that long-tenured teachers, on the average, are academically weaker than their younger colleagues, many of whom intend to remain in the profession for only a few years.

An array of theories has been advanced to explain this important and persistent phenomenon. In large part the deteriorating academic performance of the nation's students has been attributed to the fact that the teaching profession was increasingly recruited from the least able and least prepared of the country's college and university graduates. State government, and especially state education agencies, found it necessary to respond to the public's concern with consistently declining student academic performance attributed largely to poor teaching and teachers. The response of state agencies and political institutions generally took two forms. First, a variety of programs were launched to improve teacher recruitment and performance. Second and more important, state governments, and their education agencies, initiated comprehensive accountability programs that in effect significantly eroded the prerogatives and authority of classroom teachers, school building administrators, and the local school boards as well. The advent of ever-more sophisticated accountability technologies increased state funding, and public/political demands for improved educational results inevitably led to a significantly more powerful role for the states and to a correspondingly diminished role for local authorities and classroom teachers.

The capacity of state and local education authorities to improve the quality of the teaching profession was adversely affected by a protracted era of teacher shortage accentuated by an increasing availability of attractive career options for women who might otherwise have entered the teaching profession.

The persistent low-perceived status of teaching, however, may say less about the profession than it does about the relative value that American society places on the education of its youth. For a variety of reasons that must be addressed if significant educational reform is to be realized, teaching has long been a relatively unattractive career choice for the nation's more talented and academically able college graduates. As long as this antipathy to a teaching career persists, it is highly unlikely that substantial reform will occur. In 1992 it is estimated that the nation's schools will seek to recruit more than 200,000 new teachers. The projected supply is less than 138,000. When the supply of teachers is significantly less than the demand, there is a tendency for academic qualifications to fall even further, as a variety of circumventions to existing certification standards come into play. New national certification standards, as discussed above, may be in place by 1993, but if there are relatively few qualified teachers to fill the anticipated vacancies, the positions, of necessity, will be occupied by less qualified and less credentialed candidates. It is also important to note that each state, and conceivably each school system, will be free to adopt or not to adopt the new national standards. Furthermore, each state will be free to set its own passing score on the national teacher's exam. Thus, there is small likelihood that a national standard will evolve or that parents or citizens will clearly understand the relative merits of their schools. The fact that the National Certification Program is not in any way accountable to the federal government has led the U.S. Secretary of Education and members of Congress to oppose the board's request for a $25 million appropriation.

The net effect of this long-term tendency to entrust the education of our youth to those relatively less academically prepared is highlighted by the following data: "If schools of education and public school employers insisted that to be a teacher, one must score above an SAT verbal score of 496 (the mean for non-recruits), nearly 70% of those in this sample who indicated they were committed to teaching at age thirty would be denied access to the teaching profession."[9]

The relatively negative public perception of the teaching profession and the historic tendency to recruit teachers from the lower academic test levels are commented on at some length because this critically important phenomenon has changed very little over the past three decades. A 1986 survey revealed that more than a quarter of the nation's practicing teachers do not expect to remain in the profession five years hence.[10]

Those who advocate a policy of significantly enhanced teacher authority over public education should ponder well these data. It does not follow, nor is it suggested here, that enhanced teacher power is inherently an undesirable policy alternative. To the contrary, in Chapter 6 we suggest that given the right circumstances it is indeed feasible and desirable to decentralize authority, as long as it is within the context of an explicit national policy. However, before we consider turning over the ailing educational enterprise to hundreds of thousands of teachers and school building administrators, first it is necessary that we attempt to improve the profession dramatically to ensure that the preponderance of the nation's teachers and school administrators are sufficiently capable and motivated to bring about the required reforms in public education. At this writing, there is little evidence that the profession has undergone a transformation of this magnitude.

Teacher effectiveness is universally acknowledged to be the most critical variable affecting the quality of education. The argument that teacher quality and motivation are abundantly in place but are rendered ineffective by a heavy-handed top-down bureaucracy has led to a number of important teacher "empowerment" experiments.

In Dade County, Florida, one of the nation's largest and most heterogeneous school systems, forty-four schools are participating in an experimental program (School Based Management/Shared Decision Making) that significantly augments the power of teachers and school administrators to determine fundamental educational policy. Underlying the philosophy of teacher empowerment is the assumption that classroom teachers are uniquely able to ascertain the educational needs of their students and understand what must be done to minister to those needs. Given the considerable evidence describing the average teacher's level of academic preparation, performance, and commitment, one might legitimately question the operational implications of this assumption. We need to be reminded that teacher prerogatives were eroded over the past two decades in response to consistently deteriorating student performance. The past decade, characterized by the introduction of state accountability requirements that effectively limited district and building-level authority, coincides with a halt in the protracted decline in student academic performance and, more recently, with a slow but steady improvement in relevant test scores.

The governance of Dade County's experimental program varies by participating school but essentially is composed of a preponderance of teachers and senior "building" administrators, union leaders, and parents. The governing board is responsible for formulating the school budget and determining the curriculum. It plays a major role in the selection and annual evaluation of the principal. A willingness to turn over educational decision making, including the vital areas of curriculum, professional evaluation, and budget, to a building-level structure that with few exceptions has historically failed to resolve the educational problems associated with inner-city minority schools should raise considerable doubts as to the likelihood of success.

Ironically the educational establishment effectively argues against vouchers and other forms of public support for private schools on the basis that the public interest is not represented. It is difficult to comprehend how a school system composed of relatively autonomous building-level boards dominated by teachers and to a lesser extent by neighborhood parents differs much from the governance structure of private schools—a system that is perceived by the educational establishment as a denial of the public's interest in the education of the nation's youth.

An interesting variation on this approach is currently under way in Rochester, New York. The restructuring of that city's schools is also heralded as a nationally significant experiment. And indeed there are reasons to believe that this may be the case, for this pilot project is being carried out in collaboration with the newly established Rochester-based National Center for Education and the Economy. The agenda of this most recent para-private institution includes responsibility for developing concrete policy proposals to implement the major recommendations of the reform reports. The center is headed by Marc Tucker, formerly the director of the Carnegie Forum on Education and the Economy. Tucker also serves as the director of the highly publicized Rochester School Restructuring Project. The Carnegie Corporation is financially supporting this undertaking. Hopefully the involvement of the Carnegie Corporation, as well as the possibility of substantial funding by the state of New York, will suffice to spare this important national pilot project the oblivion that has been the fate of most of its equally well-intended predecessors. Unfortunately this may not be the case, for by 1989, the nationally heralded Rochester model already evidenced difficulties. The national pilot project, which provides for teacher salaries ($28 to 68,000) higher than anywhere in the United States other than Alaska, also requires that the participating teachers perform a variety of activities usually associated with professional social workers. For example, this new breed of highly paid professional is expected to visit regularly the homes of students on a scheduled basis, which in some Rochester inner-city neighborhoods is perceived as somewhat risky. In practice, the Rochester teachers have been reluctant to carry out such normally nonteaching responsibilities. Many teachers have yet to make their first visit to a student's home. Ironically, by decentralizing much of the day-to-day control over the schools to the building/teacher level, the administration has relinquished much of the authority needed to ensure conformity with the requirements of the program. Despite the high salaries, decentralized authority, and national publicity, teacher morale is reported to be low. A faction of the professional union is considering running a slate of candidates in opposition to the union leadership that supported the experiment.[11]

Major restructuring is also proposed for the Los Angeles schools, the nation's second largest system. A report containing some 612 recommendations was released late in 1988. The major sections of the report call for teacher empowerment and the development of career ladders. It recommends that less time should be spent in the classroom on rote learning, which it suggests should be relegated to homework, and more time should be devoted to discussion, simulation games, and student work groups—proposals that many of us apprehensively associate with the "progressive" 1960s.

Only in the United States is it conceivable that two of the nation's four largest school systems, in splendid isolation, set out to radically restructure "American" education. The Los Angeles plan, tacitly acknowledging that the United States shares a common core of beliefs, recommends the inclusion of twenty-six such values, modestly offered as the essence of the nation's fundamental ideology, as an integral part of its restructured curriculum and school system.

The banner of teacher empowerment has been unfurled by the two major unions. At its July 1988 national convention the American Federation of Teachers went on record in support of the cause. President Albert Shanker proposed "that local school boards and unions jointly develop a procedure that would enable teachers and others, to submit and implement proposals to set up their own autonomous public schools within their school buildings."[12] One might well ponder whether "autonomous public school" is a contradiction in terms. President Shanker led the struggle against the takeover of the Chelsea public schools system by Boston University. He properly asks if such a turnover is constitutional. "Can an

elected public body turn everything over to a private institution?"[13]
Would not the autonomous public schools suggested by Shanker
constitute a comparable abdication of public responsibility?

The NEA has also boarded the empowered teachers bandwagon.
Mary Hatwood Futrell, addressing her fellow teachers as they
convened in 1988 in New Orleans, spoke from a script similar to
Shanker's. In a widely circulated document, she urged that experimental special school districts be established that would provide
for more flexible scheduling, partnerships with area colleges,
financing by means other than property taxes, and curriculums
managed by classroom teachers.[14] Nor does Futrell see much of a
rule for traditional public institutions. She suggests that the substance of the restructuring be determined by teachers, administrators, parents, and the business community.

Possibly the most radical policy to empower teachers further
and decentralize education to the community level occurred in
Chicago in 1988–89. In what may have been a case of political
weariness and frustration the Illinois legislature voted to permit
radical restructuring of Chicago's school system, the third largest
in the nation. Proposed is the establishment of 594 local parent
councils, one for each of the city's schools. The projected school
councils are to be composed of ten elected members: six parents,
two teachers, and two neighborhood residents without children in
that school. The council would have extraordinary power—so
much so that it is difficult to see how curriculum uniformity or
standards would be assured. Each of the 594 councils would be
given authority to hire and fire the principal, to control the budget,
and to develop the educational plan. It is ironic that at the very
same moment New York City is critically examining its 1969
community-based decentralization policy, with a view either to
abandoning the approach or to significantly curtailing the autonomy of community boards. Chicago is moving in exactly the
opposite direction. The ideal of community power and involvement proscribed by the educational/academic establishment in
1968 for New York's ailing school system remains an elusive
phantom.

As commented on at greater length above, New York's thirty-two, nine-member community school boards did not, as intended, generate substantial interest in or an abiding concern for the city schools on the part of Hispanic and black parents. The idealized participatory democratic community governance never material-ized, and the concept remains essentially a romantic unworkable theory advanced by the educational/academic establishment as a model remedy to the nation's educational crisis. Hopefully a lesson has been learned, for if not, history may repeat itself at enormous costs to the nation's poor and predominantly minority children.

The nation's four largest school systems enrolling the greater part of the country's black and Hispanic students, with little if any evidence of coordination, are in the process of fundamentally restructuring their schools and in radically different ways. What occurs—and more important, what does not occur—in the nation's four largest school systems will go far in determining whether impoverished inner-city, predominantly minority youth will, or will not, enter the mainstream of American society and culture and thereby significantly influence the future of the United States. That this process is occurring in the absence of any planned national input or coordination does not augur well for the nation.

In a democracy the public expresses its interpretation of and agreement with its fundamental values through the political/electoral processes. Yet a number of influential scholars vehemently ques-tion the wisdom of involving citizen-elected governmental insti-tutions in the formulation of educational policy. Joel Spring, an articulate liberal scholar who has written extensively on educa-tional policy-making, for example, advises that

> until the federal government and the state legislatures stop making curriculum changes on the basis of social, political and economic needs, the curriculum of the public schools will continue to be in a state of ... chaos. ... In a democratic society the answer to that central question [what knowledge is of most worth] should be given by individuals, not by governments.[15]

If this indeed is the case, then what is the meaning of public school or of the common school?

Chapter 5 concludes with a brief presentation of a few reform-related "unconventional" concepts, included not as much in advocacy as in illustration of the range of alternative strategies possible when relatively more fundamental questions are posed.

SOME NOT-SO-COMMON POLICY ALTERNATIVES

A Fourth Branch of Government

Possibly the most intriguing, if not particularly practical, proposal for bringing about fundamental reform in the nation's educational enterprise is one suggested by Spring. Convinced that the existing system encourages excessive influence on the part of major political and economic interest groups, and that local public control (read "local schools boards") is often a vehicle for maintaining the status quo, Spring suggests that consideration be given to amending the Constitution to provide for a fourth branch of government assigned responsibility for "public schooling . . . with the same protection from outside influences that is given to the Supreme Court."[16]

For a moment one might conclude that Spring, who has consistently argued against a significant role in education for formal governmental institutions, possibly had experienced a fundamental change of heart. However, on closer examination this proves not to be the case; for in the next breath, he recommends that control of "the fourth branch of government should be given to a board of teachers who would be appointed for life by members of the teaching profession."[17] Any resemblance here to a Supreme Court whose members are appointed by an elected president and require confirmation by an elected U.S. Senate exists—but in the eyes of the beholder. Ironically, while opposing a substantial role for public institutions in educational policy-making, the educational establishment and academe experience little difficulty suggesting that an essentially para-private, publicly unaccountable national policy process be entrusted with the education of the nation's children.

The Physiology of Learning

A second not-so-common alternative is less concerned with restructuring schools, or reforming the teaching profession, than it is with scientifically exploring the learning process. The variety of studies and approaches to this still imprecisely defined field are most likely to emanate from the work of the neuro- and the bio-behavioral sciences than from schools of education. Recent advances in scientific instrumentation and capacity to "model" have provided new means to study how learning occurs or, just as important, does not occur. As a state commissioner of education for some dozen years, this writer has observed the flow of millions of dollars of research funding for the intended purposes of acquiring a better understanding of subjects such as, What makes for an effective school? Teacher? Classroom? Curriculum? Few would argue that the product of these three decades of considerable public expenditure for educational research has been substantial. If but 10 percent of available educational research funding had been committed to what we here term "the physiology of learning," we might today be much better equipped to formulate and implement viable and instrumentally effective alternative educational policies.

As early as 1980, for example, the scientific community knew not only that lead was a dangerous substance that especially poor children might likely ingest from flaking paint but also that lead was associated with different aspects of intelligence as measured by performance on IQ tests.[18]

Increasingly, data suggest that the interaction of environmental influences and physiological factors such as diet are critical to a comprehension of learning and related behavior. We know from research in this country and in the developing world not only that malnutrition affects learning at the time of deprivation but that in infants it leads to important structural changes in the brain. We also have long been aware of the relationship of exercise to corresponding changes in the cell structure of muscle. Thus, it is not surprising that "behavior" can also bring about changes in other organs such as the brain. Indeed, one of the most significant factors emerging from contemporary research in the pharmacological neuro- and bio-behavioral sciences is the interdependence of learning and related physiological changes in the brain. It is conceivable that the relative decline in American economic productivity, which the major reform reports are inclined to lay at the doorstep of the public schools, may be less attributable to bad science education than to the absence of a comprehensive national prenatal and early child-care policy.

Today it is generally acknowledged that a nutritionally sound diet does enhance a child's learning capability. "Nutrition," in this context, generally refers to certain foods that we have reason to believe positively or negatively affect learning or related behaviors. The extraordinary advances in scientific instrumentation that have occurred in recent years increasingly make it possible to determine precisely the chemical attributes of foods that impact cell structures and how. To the extent to which this is the case it is increasingly possible to extract such substances or to synthesize them in the laboratory. For example, recent experiments strongly suggest that vasopressin analog (DDAVP) impacts on the learning capability of human beings. This peptide "causes a general improvement in ability to learn the required discriminations. . . . [The] group treated with DDAVP solved all problems significantly faster than either placebo or no treatment control groups."[19] Other experiments suggest that "attentional function may be peptide-specific."[20]

All teachers are sensitive to the wide variation in attention span and learning style that characterizes their students. Relatively little consideration, however, has been devoted to the extent to which these important differences correlate with variations in the brain and how effective intervention strategies might conceivably be developed. Available data show a correlation, for example, between group and individual differences and variations in normal brain organization. A variation of PET scanners makes it possible to develop what are in effect unique "brain prints." This technology enables scientists to detect metabolic changes occurring in the brain.

Today it is possible to correlate specific behaviors with specific brain activity and associated neurotransmitters. The cellular identification of characteristics associated with specific behaviors need not necessarily be determined through analysis of brain tissue—a near impossibility in the case of human beings—but increasingly can be identified in cells located elsewhere, for example, in blood or urine.

We know that left- or right-handedness and sex correlate with differing organizations of the brain: "Handedness differences are reliably associated with differences in cognitive abilities, but in complex ways that depend on sex, reasoning level, . . ."[21] The research of Richard Harshman, Elizabeth Hampson, and Sheri Berenbaum has led them to conclude that "there may be many different kinds of normal brain organization, each with its own cognitive advantages and disadvantages."[22] If this proposition is valid and to the extent to which research permits the identification of specific characteristics of the many types of brain organization, it is potentially possible to develop a most powerful pedagogy that might conceivably make far-reaching contributions to remedying the problems confronting learning, under a variety of differing conditions.

Studies of alcoholism in humans and other behaviorisms in animals suggest the existence of important genetically determined predisposition to behave in predictable ways. More important, however, is the growing understanding of the relationship between environmental factors such as stress, fear, or boredom and the extent to which latent predispositions are manifested. Thus, it is conceivable, on the average, that genetically similar youngsters might behave in radically different ways, depending on the quality of their immediate environment. Then it follows that children and youth having to cope with the environmental conditions associated with life in the urban ghetto and rural slum are more likely to manifest latent behavior patterns than their genetically similar counterparts living in the relative security of affluent suburbia.

We are all genetically predisposed to certain behavioral characteristics. Whether these behavioral predispositions, the good and the bad, become manifest is in important part determined by the quality of our environment. Thus, to the extent that it is possible to control a child's environment, either by exposing the youngster to an alternative setting or by altering the elements that define his or her environment, though deliberate public policy, it is theoretically possible to minimize undesirable behaviors and to maximize desirable ones. Such logic argues strongly in favor of comprehensive child and youth policies, as opposed to concentration on school and schooling reform strategies.

Surely the scientific progress made in this vital area in recent years deserves a fraction of the millions of dollars that flow annually to finance orthodox research that to date has produced but marginal improvements in schools and schooling. Unfortunately the educational establishment is relatively ignorant of the important research that is currently under way in this area and of the enormous potential it holds for the educational enterprise.

Undoubtedly the spectacular advances that have been made in the neurosciences in recent years will significantly affect our understanding of variable intelligences and the human behavior that is called "learning." The relative paucity of complex, stimulating experiences that characterizes growing up in cultural poverty not only influences youngsters' immediate behavior but, more importantly, affects their ultimate behavioral potential. For example, animal tests indicate that a depletion of "dopamine" to the prefrontal cortex produces a negative effect on memory and other types of cognitive skills. We are also aware that certain substances can increase or decrease the amount of dopamine that is available to the brain. In addition, we know that brain cells, not unlike other body cells, trade molecules in a complex but now understood way that permits the flow of important messages affecting not only momentary but subsequent behavior as well. It is called *learning*!

Critical to this process are the junctions in the brain, "synapses." By generating new synapses the brain can change in response to experience. Research at the University of Illinois, for example, shows that rats raised in mentally stimulating environments develop more synapses than those that lead duller lives. Learning and experience "influence behavior and the ultimate potential for behavior. They do these things by affecting the strength of synaptic transmission" and produce long-lasting changes in behavior.[23] Jon Franklin in his fascinating book *Molecules of the Mind* sums it up as follows:

> Behind every thought or feeling, there was a molecular reaction in the brain. Behind every molecule in the reaction, there was an enzyme that created that molecule; behind every enzyme was a gene. If the gene was defective (or triggered by the environment), the enzyme was defective, so would be the molecule; if the molecule was defective so would be the chemical reaction and so inevitably, would be the thought and the reaction produced.[24]

Increasingly research points to a critically important relationship between normal development of the nervous system and availability of relevant stimuli. Current policy—or more precisely, the absence of policy—therefore not only deprives millions of inner-city and rural slum minority youngsters of an equal educational opportunity but in effect physiologically predisposes them to a life sentence in the permanent underclass. The nation's stake in this issue is indeed high.

Every technology that helps us to understand better the manner in which the brain, body, and experience interact to affect our "life chances" significantly will inevitably impact society. Unfortunately a tradition of disdain and suspicion concerning the role of technology and science have characterized the educational profession, with the chilling consequence of casting inquiries and research in the general area of the "physiology of learning" into the "verboten" arena. Unless those concerned about and responsible for the evolution of policy alternatives capable of reversing the downward cycle in American education are bold and audacious enough to study and comprehend this critically important dimension, and assuredly others equally as unorthodox, we may be doomed to an eternity of mediocrity.

NOTES

1. Michael W. Kirst, "Sustaining the Momentum of State Education Reform: The Link between Assessment and Financial Support," *Phi Delta Kappan* 67:5 (January 1986): 343.

2. Lucia Solorzano, "Teaching in Trouble," *U.S. News & World Report* 100:20 (26 May 1986): 52.

3. Susan J. Rosenholtz, "Political Myths about Educational Reform: Lessons from Research on Teaching," *Phi Delta Kappan* 66:5 (January 1985): 350.

4. Harold Hodgkinson, *All One System: Demographics of Education, Kindergarten through Graduate School* (Washington, D.C.: Institute for Educational Leadership, 1985), 11.

5. Rosenholtz, "Political Myths," 351.

6. Myron Liberman, *Beyond Public Education* (New York: Praeger, 1986), 2.

7. Ernest Boyer, quoted in Edward B. Fiske, "U.S. Testing of Students Raises Growing Debate," *New York Times*, 27 December 1987, I:28.

8. Victor S. Vance and Philip C. Schlechty, *The Structure of the Teaching Occupation and the Characteristics of Teachers* (Washington, D.C.: National Institute of Education 81-0100, 1981), 188.

9. Ibid., 29.

10. Solorzano, "Teaching in Trouble," 52.

11. "A Fair Chance for Young Black Men," *New York Times*, 4 April 1989, I:26.

12. Albert Shanker, "Convention Plots New Course," *New York Times*, 10 July 1988, IV:7.

13. Albert Shanker, "Questions for a University President," *New York Times*, 11 December 1988, E:7.

14. "Teachers' Union Backs Plan for Special Districts," *New York Times*, 5 July 1988, I:15.

15. Joel Spring, "Education and the SONY Wars," *Phi Delta Kappan* 65:8(April 1984): 537.

16. Joel Spring, *Conflict of Interest: The Politics of American Education* (New York: Longman, 1988), 180.

17. Ibid.

18. R. W. Thatcher et al., "Effects of Low Levels of Cadmium and Lead on Cognitive Functioning in Children," *Archives of Environmental Health* 37:3 (May-June 1982): 164.

19. Bill E. Beckwith et al., "Vasopressin Analog (DDAVP) Facilitates Conceptual Learning in Human Males," *Peptides* 3:4 (1982): 628.

20. Curt Sandman et al., "Are Learning and Attention Related to the Sequence of Amino-Acids in ACTH-MSH Peptides?," *Peptides* 1:4 (1980): 280.

21. Richard Harshman, Elizabeth Hampson, and Sheri A. Berenbaum, "Individual Differences in Cognitive Abilities and Brain Organization, Part 1. Sex and Handedness Differences in Ability," *Canadian Journal of Psychology* 37:1 (March 1983): 180.

22. Ibid.

23. Morton F. Reiser, *Mind, Brain, Body: Toward Convergence of Psychoanalysis and Neurobiology* (New York: Basic Books, 1984), 105.

24. Jon Franklin, *Molecules of the Mind: The Brave New Science of Molecular Psychology* (New York: Atheneum, 1987), 146.

6

A National Public Policy Process

The current approach to resolving what is universally acknowledged to be a national education/youth crisis is ineffective and incapable of bringing about critically required reform. The federal nature of the American Constitution, reinforced by a long tradition of local control and states' rights, has limited the central government's involvement in the education of America's children and youth to a marginal and relatively insignificant role. As long as the education of the nation's youth was not a matter significantly affecting the national interest, an essentially anarchic and chaotic educational policy process was adequate and maybe even appropriate. Few would argue, however, that the quality and equity of education and other youth and child services today are not critical to the national interest. It is increasingly imperative that a more rational and effective policy process be developed.

Over the past century the absence of a national public policy process has contributed to the gradual evolution of a para-private network of institutions and associations that in effect have initiated and implemented much of the national educational policy that exists. An overlapping association of academics (and especially those from a few select universities) with a variety of para-private foundations, institutes, and related associations has evolved during much of this century to a point that it essentially constitutes the nation's educational policy process and establishment. The nation is indebted to the many individuals and institutions who, in the absence of a national policy process, assumed responsibility for addressing what they accurately perceived to be increasingly national educational needs—needs not susceptible to being addressed by an array of relatively autonomous states and school districts. However, this para-private policy process, by definition, is incapable of being publicly accountable. Furthermore, its existence and composition have had the effect of framing critical national issues in relatively narrow school and schooling parameters. Therefore, it has tended to neglect the more comprehensive and serious crisis afflicting the nation's poor and predominantly minority youth and children. Required is a revised educational policy process that is both national and publicly accountable. The concluding thoughts that follow suggest some possible alternatives to the many school and schooling solutions proposed by the numerous reform studies analyzed in the previous chapter.

But before sketching some alternative strategies, it is necessary to assess the possible consequences of a perpetuation of current policies.

IMPLICATIONS OF A FAILED REFORM PROCESS

The volatile nature of the current debate over the quality and purposes of public education is a predictable response to the accelerating tempo of change. In the days that the son was likely to walk in the footsteps of the father, the lessons of the latter were sufficient to the education of the former. However, when the magnitude of the changes spanning a single generation is greater than that of the entire century, conflict over who should be educated, by whose authority, to what purpose, and at what and whose expense is inevitable and likely to be protracted and intense.

Ours is an aging society. With the exception of its minorities, it is a society that enrolls fewer and fewer children in the public schools. A willingness to undergo taxation to fund education is partly determined by one's economic status but also by the number of one's children attending public schools. It also is related to the extent to which the taxpayer perceives education to be personally and/or socially valuable. Surely the persistence of human society and civilization attests to an adult generation's realization that socialization and education of children are requisite to immortality. However, the intensity of child advocacy that characterizes a people at a given moment in history is capable of considerable variation. Support for public schools, for example, was high during the 1950s and 1960s, an era in which most American families had children attending the nation's public schools. Relative economic affluence also strengthened the inclination of tax-paying parents to support school tax levies, budgets, and bond issues. Today's society, however, increasingly consists of an aging population, often subsisting on an inflation-vulnerable fixed income. What it all adds up to is that when fewer and fewer adults, for whatever reason, cease to view public education or educators favorably, child advocacy is the victim.

Also impacting on the viability of possible educational reform is the tendency in many cities and some impoverished rural areas for the ethnic and/or racial composition of the power structure to differ radically from that of the relatively powerless consumers of the bulk of the educational services. Given the decentralized nature of the governance structure, it is not uncommon in such situations for a mayor, board, or council to represent more the interests of an aging, white voting constituency than those of the ethnic or racial minorities enrolling the greater part of the children in the schools. The reluctance of such polities to levy taxes to support the education of "other people's children"—children often of a different color, speaking an "alien" language—inclines the advocates of the powerless to turn to the state or federal government for redress.

The failure of a highly decentralized policy process to advocate, or even to represent, the interests of children also occurs as a consequence of the uneven geographic distribution of older citizens. Traditionally the local school district, as the primary agent of governance, served society well. Historically most school districts were relatively homogeneous. The near demise of the traditional extended family, social security benefits, retirement plans, and rapid and inexpensive transportation have inclined a growing number of the nation's senior citizens to relocate and establish their own homogeneous, relatively childless communities. Thus, it is not uncommon for the governance of a growing number of school jurisdictions to be dominated by local majorities of senior citizens. As most live on a fixed, inflation-vulnerable income in communities where few, if any, of the children in the schools are theirs or even their grandchildren, there exists a powerful incentive to curtail and to minimize support for public education, thus furthering the inequity of educational and other child and youth services.

An additional factor mitigating against even marginal national educational reform is the conservative philosophy of the Reagan years, a philosophy that argued that public educational policymaking had no rightful place in Washington and should be returned to the states and localities where it properly belongs. It was further contended that the myriad of federal categorical educational programs and attendant dollars, which cumbersomely sought to substitute for a national educational policy, be replaced by block grants, which would permit state and local authorities, rather than Washington, to determine the beneficiaries of federal dollars.

This conservative ideology also advocated that educational decision making, to the extent possible, be removed entirely from the public sector and be left the prerogative of the parents. The burgeoning movement for enlarged subsidies for nonpublic schools, for vouchers, and for tuition tax credits is indicative of both a desire to decentralize educational decision making and an intent to require that the beneficiaries of education, rather than the community at large, bear the primary burden.

A subtle but significant change in the expectations that Americans hold for their public schools shapes these changing values. Our forefathers believed that public schools could and would provide the ladder enabling successive generations of poor, ethnic, and minority children to climb out of the ghetto and assimilate into the dominant culture. Although this belief was partially an aspect of the nation's political mythology, it represented reality as well. Contemporary Americans, however, are not as inclined to believe that the public schools are capable of this assignment. More ominous is a growing sense that this goal not only is impossible to achieve but perhaps is not even a desirable end.

The persistent failure of our public schools to successfully address the educational needs of most black and Hispanic children contrasts markedly to the historic role of schools and schooling in economic and social advancement. The failure of schools to deliver economic and social liberation has discouraged black and Hispanic parents from motivating their children to stay in school. Their limited educational achievement, ignorance of the "system," and lack of confidence in the school's ability or intent to fulfill its traditional mission render them relatively powerless and politically enfeebled. Powerlessness begets powerlessness; in the United States our rapidly growing population of poor minority children are particularly powerless.

Lowered expectations about what the schools can or should do are vividly portrayed by the qualitative decline in the quality of the educational professions, analyzed at some length in Chapter 5. A people that consistently and consciously condones a policy process that each year sends less and less academically able and prepared teachers into the classrooms obviously does not expect that public education will accomplish its historic assignment—surely a self-fulfilling prophecy. As the quality of those entering the teaching profession falls, as the most talented leave for more rewarding and respected employment, the capacity of the system to fulfill its assigned mission even minimally is correspondingly eroded, which in turn gives credence to public and media criticism, lower budgets, and declining levels of student performance. Such is the vicious cycle that has characterized public education in the United States for the latter years of this century. Unless this tenacious cycle of lowered expectations, lowered support, and declining performance can be arrested, it is not likely that public education, as we have known it over the past century, will survive. That cycle cannot be broken and reversed, short of fundamental changes in the educational policy process.

The traditional governance structure consisting of some 16,000 semiautonomous school districts, regulated with varying degrees and effectiveness by fifty state governments, marginally impacted by the federal government, and sporadically channeled by a para-private network of foundations and related institutions, is inadequate to the task of arresting and reversing this catastrophic cycle. Unless it is recognized at the highest levels of government that the crisis is national in its dimensions and affects the total life of the nation's poor children and youth, what is likely to occur is the emergence of a tripartite school system, with sobering implications for the future of our society.

THE SPECTER OF A TRIPARTITE SCHOOL SYSTEM

Relatively wealthy suburban schools essentially segregated by race and/or class will become more and more independent of the larger system, as educational policy-making is more and more devolved to the district and even to the school building level. Inner-city and poor rural schools increasingly will be funded and controlled by state agencies as they move to implement recently acquired authority to take over "bankrupt" schools—schools that also will be highly segregated by race and class. And last, if dissatisfaction with the public schools, fueled by a continued decline in most measures of student and/or teacher performance, continues to grow, the resultant increased demand for vouchers and tuition tax credits in support of nonpublic schools will trigger a substantial increase in the number of students attending private schools, also segregated by race and class and, by definition, publicly unaccountable.

If this is indeed a possible scenario, it is conceivable that within a decade or two the nation's educational system could be characterized by (1) urban and poor rural schools, mostly black and

Hispanic, controlled and governed by state governments, many dominated by suburban white legislators and officials; (2) suburban schools, increasingly freed from state and even from district controls, resembling more the publicly nonaccountable private school system than the urban/poor rural public sector; and (3) a relatively large private school system subsidized by vouchers, tax credits, and the like.

Thus might this polyglot nation, bereft of the cohesion of a national religion or of centuries of a shared homogeneous culture, come to educate and socialize its children in radically differing ways. While each of these tripartite systems might conceivably educate its clients equally well, albeit separately, and in the process effectively inculcate its respective values and mores, where and how will vital national interests be addressed, the interests for which Henry Barnard a century ago prescribed the imperative of "the common school"?

Is it conceivable that the nation's educational system, traditionally perceived as the fuel firing the melting pot, might become more a divisive than a unifying force in American society? Will the nation's schools, long regarded as the conveyor belt of ethnic and class mobility, in reality contribute to the realization of a permanent underclass and an attendant subculture? Will an emergent tripartite school system further the erosion of a social conscience requisite to national sensitivity and thus diminish the national will to make the sacrifices that will be necessary to avert this impending national calamity?

In less than a generation, today's minority public school population will likely become the majority. Unless the dangerous cycle, described above, is confronted and reversed, it will not be possible for this nation to compete effectively economically or militarily in an increasingly global and interdependent world. Unless the existing policy process, which perpetuates a system of racial and class isolation with its attendant hostility and suspicion, is altered, it is not likely that the nation will maintain the degree of social cohesion and tolerance necessary to sustain its traditional democracy.

SOME ALTERNATIVE POLICY APPROACHES

To suggest that the existing policy process is no longer adequate and must be seriously revamped if public education is to survive is to tread a mine field! Nonetheless, some two decades of labor in the educational vineyard and in pondering and attempting to comprehend what has and has not occurred has led me to conclude that such a journey must be attempted.

The fundamental problems are quite apparent, although many would seek to avoid them. The nation is experiencing a most serious crisis, in large part attributable to the inadequacies of its existing educational policy processes. The general decline in student performance, as measured by a variety of standardized tests, and as compared with the performance of comparable youngsters in developed countries abroad, augurs ill for the nation's economic well-being and for the national security. More serious, but less appreciated, are the implications of the rapidly changing racial and ethnic demographics of the nation's youth. Our future adult citizenry, to whom, of necessity, we must look to sustain the nation's economy, culture, and civility, is increasingly composed of black and Hispanic youth, a youth, however, that is more and more locked into dead-end, inescapable rural and urban ghettos.

The challenge is to devise an alternative policy process that can at the same time maintain, indeed enhance, local/teacher initiatives and authority, while entrusting the federal government with responsibility for addressing, in an authoritative and public manner, the national education/youth crisis. At the very outset any attempt to confront this sensitive issue will require a degree of political courage and dexterity sufficient to overcome the deeply ingrained national phobia concerning a more-than-marginal role for the federal government in educational policy-making.

Even an oblique suggestion that the federal role in educational policy-making be enhanced commensurate with the national dimensions of the acknowledged crisis is carefully and studiously avoided by most politicians. The 1988 presidential campaign, more so than any before, was required to address the issue of education. Concern about the plight of the nation's youth, whether expressed in terms of education, child care, teenage delinquency, and pregnancy or in terms of minority youth unemployment and drop-out rate, ranked near the top of the public's list of critically important issues that it believed the 1988 presidential campaign should address. However, the candidates were about as disinclined to grapple with this issue as with the deficit. Although the dreaded "T" word ("tax") was obviously a factor, political sensitivity to the existence of potentially campaign-debilitating jurisdictional mine fields probably better explains the reluctance to deal with these issues in other than a rhetorical and superficial manner.

Vice President Bush did not wait for either the election returns or his inauguration to begin to chisel his ideal political epitaph. "I want to be known as the Education President!" Why this extraordinary concern, by the next president of the United States, for an institution that since the earliest days of the Republic has been zealously reserved to the states and localities? The president elect may not go down in history as another great communicator, but few would challenge his ability to sense correctly the issues troubling his fellow Americans; he no doubt was keenly aware that the opinion polls documented an American people increasingly worried about the deteriorating quality of public education.

Public opinion polls and the media gave the candidates little choice but to deal with this thorny issue, and both party platforms contained language outlining proposed strategies to address this vital matter. Predictably the Republican platform promised tuition tax credits in support of private education, urged states to legislate voucher programs, and went on record in favor of educational decisions being made primarily by parents, then by the communities, and finally, if necessary, by the states. The Democratic platform, equally as predictably, advocated significantly increased funding for education, with a particular emphasis on targeting services to the economically disadvantaged and the handicapped. Both candidates were careful to ensure that their interests in education did not translate into advocacy for changes in the role of the federal government. In a major campaign speech Vice President Bush did not leave his audience in doubt about his commitment to the orthodoxy of local control:

> When it comes to better schools, almost all of the wisdom and good answers, and the money to pay the bills should come from outside Washington, D.C. . . . There is much on our national agenda for education, and most of it must happen at the state and local levels, which provide 93% of the financial support, which they should."[1]

Leon Botstein, president of Bard College, reacting to the dearth of comprehensive educational proposals in the 1988 campaign rhetoric, commented appropriately:

> Despite five years of reports and debates, as well as moralistic rhetoric from the Reagan administration, the quality of our schools continues to decline. Yet the Presidential candidates offer Band-Aids and gimmicks. They seem scared of the costs and the public's reaction to any federal initiative. They lack the courage to argue that federal money can be invested without giving up local control. . . . What is at stake is nothing less than our economic well being, our national security, and the quality of our culture and daily lives.[2]

The narrow focus on school and schooling issues, along with an attendant bias against an enhanced role for the federal government, contributes to the persistence of relatively impotent administrative and legislative institutions. Because political institutions at the federal level labor under the correct assumption that Washington's role in public education is but minor and marginal, policy is rarely initiated in response to the interests of children and youth but rather in response to more "legitimate" concerns such as national security, unemployment, drugs, crime, and AIDS.

Membership on education committees, except for the few but notable members of Congress who have demonstrated a particular interest in this area, is rarely highly prized. The education bureaucracy's influence on the administration and Congress traditionally has been relatively weak. The education policy vacuum at the national level led Samuel Halperin, an insightful scholar and experienced bureaucrat, to conclude that "there is no coherent, widely shared, or clearly understood 'national policy' for supporting or strengthening the abstraction called 'the nation's educational system.' . . . What is missing . . . is a national strategy for strengthening policy making in education."[3]

Nor have the many influential educational interest groups contributed significantly to integrating and focusing youth- and child-related issues. The preoccupation of the myriad of educational associations with their own specific interests, and with the seeming specter of "federal control," has tended to render them far less influential than their numbers and power would imply. The narrow concern with schools and schooling has occasionally led education associations to oppose legislation directed to the provision of youth services, fearing that the attendant resources would come at their expense or that the proposed services would be provided by a potentially rival institution. It would appear that a more focused and targeted policy process is required.

A WHITE HOUSE CONFERENCE
ON CHILDREN AND YOUTH

The Bush administration might usefully familiarize itself with the strategy adopted by President Dwight Eisenhower in 1952 when faced with a somewhat comparable situation and convene a major White House conference on children and youth. However, it will be necessary to avoid the temptation of limiting such a conference to education or to governors as President Bush did in September 1989, and to the educational establishment, for the fundamental issue is not simply an education crisis but one that afflicts the total environment impacting on the lives of the nation's children and youth, and especially its disadvantaged minority children and youth. For this reason it is critically important that such a conference be attended by persons experienced and knowledgeable in such diverse areas as prenatal and early childhood development, health and nutrition, youth policy, alternative modes and institutions for learning, the physiology and chemistry of learning, and juvenile justice.

The agenda for such a White House conference would need to be meticulously crafted and should include a careful, dispassionate consideration of the role of the federal government in a restructured system of public education. Recommendations on this vital matter would benefit from the wisdom of constitutional authorities and from relevant experience abroad. If the recommendations of a White House conference as proposed in this study are to be addressed seriously, it would also be necessary that the president publicly commit his intention of submitting a relevant legislative package to the Congress by a specific date. President Bush's stated intent of an early meeting with renowned educators, business leaders, and governors unfortunately is likely to conclude in but more advocacy of business as usual.

Ideally a White House conference would culminate in legislation that would provide for a comprehensive Department of Youth and Child Services charged with a much broader range of responsibility than the existing Department of Education, including a comprehensive policy for prenatal, early childhood, and child care. Given the impotence of existing political and administrative processes, it is most important that a White House conference, as conceived here, recommend the aggregation of all existing and proposed youth- and child-related services, including education, into a new cabinet-level Department of Youth and Child Services. If the nation, because of the crisis afflicting its poor and predominantly minority children and youth, is indeed at risk, then anything less than cabinet-level responsibility will not suffice. Unlike the existing Department of Education, the proposed Department of Youth and Child Services should be charged with responsibility for assisting the administration and Congress in the development of legislation addressing the holistic problem facing the nation's children and youth. Rather than being merely supplemental to state policy or categorical in nature, federal legislation should be general and authoritative. Federal support of education, as well as other child and youth services, should be across the board, provided to the states on a per pupil formula basis according to measures of relative wealth and need. Despite mounting evidence that the American public is prepared to support a more proactive federal role in educational policy making, President Bush, in September 1989, convened a White House Conference on Education. However, the fact that participation was limited to the nation's fifty governors suggests that the current administration is determined to abide by the tenets of the conventional political liturgy, that enshrines local/state responsibility, and a narrowly circumscribed and marginal role for the federal government.

A PRENATAL, EARLY CHILDHOOD, AND CHILD-CARE POLICY

The current controversy and escalating public concern over child-care services and the ensuing rhetorical political responses are indicative of the confusion resulting from the absence of a relevant national policy process.

Some in the educational establishment support a federal role in the provision of expanded child care provided such services are incorporated within the state/local educational governance structure. But for many, any significant federal role in the provision of child care services immediately raises the specter of creeping national control. The traditional procedure employed to avoid jurisdictional conflicts of this nature is to grant federal funds to the states and/or localities to supplement their own programs. However, experience demonstrates that services, if the states chose to provide them at all, are unequal, and therefore not likely to constitute a truly national response to a perceived national crisis.

The Great Society programs of the 1960s sought to avoid jurisdictional disputes with state and local authorities by funneling program funds, whenever possible, through ad hoc community agencies. In retrospect this approach also left much to be desired.

All too frequently the targeted clients received less of the benefits than intended. The myriad of community agencies were often inefficient, disorganized, and corrupt.

Required is a nationally legislated policy on child care that specifies broad required federal standards accompanied by per capita formula funding to the states. The costs will not be inconsequential and will undoubtedly raise the dreaded specter of additional taxation. However, the long-run consequences of ignoring the needs of a rapidly growing population of poor and neglected very young children are immensely more costly. The House Select Committee on Children, Youth and Families, for example, both documented the substantial costs that the nation would incur if prenatal and early childhood services are not made available and pointed out that $1 invested in WIC (Special Supplemental Food Program for Women, Infants and Children) can save $3 in short-term hospital costs; $1 spent on preschool education can save $4.75 in subsequent social costs.

A national policy in this crucial area, to be carried out at state and local levels, will require that efficient administrative and fiscal institutions be in place. Federal policy, as suggested above, should require, and then assist the states to develop, new local governance and administrative capabilities to manage public prenatal, infant, and early childhood services. An administrative structure distinct from either the public school system or the traditional community agency is suggested for two reasons. First, by putting considerable distance between the provision of direct federal assistance to children and the public school system, it will be possible to minimize the real and imagined constitutional issues. Second, the narrow school and schooling preoccupation that characterizes the educational establishment makes it highly unlikely that the broad range of developmental needs of very young and yet-to-be-born children would be met. Obviously, close coordination and even the sharing of facilities and other resources between the public school system and relevant community agencies, as well as those residing with the proposed structure for infant and child development, will be required.

A NATIONAL EDUCATIONAL POLICY

A proactive federal role in public education would require legislation specifying precise national requirements and standards. Obviously efforts to move in this direction will be controversial. One possible place to start might be to examine a number of national nonbinding policies that have been put in place over the years by the para-private policy process. For example, the currently proposed national voluntary standards for teacher education and certification might be mandated by appropriate federal legislation. If so, the federal requirements should be general in nature and inclusive only of standards and requirements dictated by broadly conceived national interests. The public may be more inclined to support such a role for the federal government than is generally realized. A 1987 survey of public attitudes toward education reported in the September 1987 *Phi Delta Kappan* found that 84 percent of the Americans surveyed supported the federal government's involvement in ensuring that state and local educational agencies meet nationally set minimum standards. Seventy-six percent of the respondents indicated their support for a national testing program.[4] The 1989 Gallup poll portrays a continuing trend toward support for an enhanced policy role for the federal government. Once again the American people have demonstrated that they are more sensitive to the magnitude of the crisis afflicting American youth, and more inclined to look to the federal government for remedies than are those entrusted with responsibility for making educational policy. Seventy percent of the American public said that they favored "requiring the public schools in . . . [their] community to conform to national achievement standards and goals." Possibly more revealing of the gap separating the views of the public from policymakers and politicians is the fact that only 19 percent of the Gallup sample opposed national standards and curriculum.[5]

To ensure that all American youth completing public education share a minimal common learning experience and level of academic attainment commensurate with the national interest, it is not necessary to embrace a national school curriculum. Nor, as many are inclined to argue, will an enhanced federal role inevitably lead to a national curriculum. The debate over this issue obscures the fact that in many respects the curriculum is already nationalized. The national market in textbooks and tests has gone a long way to standardize what is taught, when, and to what academic level. What is lacking, however, is an explicit authoritative public policy establishing the academic and other standards required by the national interest.

Fundamental decisions as to what it is believed our youth need to know and to be able to do to ensure their own future, as well as that of the nation, of necessity will be made by someone, somehow, at some level of governance. The critical question is, Which decisions should be made by whom and at what level? For the nation, state, and community, as well as parents, have a vital interest and a critical stake in the education and socialization of our youth and the welfare of our children. A public policy process that seeks to address this reality should systematically attempt to delineate explicitly and with as much precision as possible, the areas of respective interest and responsibility. Obviously agreement as to where authority and responsibility should rest for the various aspects of the educational process will not be easily obtained. However, consensus as to the imminence and the magnitude of this national crisis hopefully will incline those involved in the debate to attempt to put aside parochial priorities and work together to identify vital interests at each level of involvement and responsibility. For example, the national interest might require that all high school graduates, regardless of which of the fifty states or 16,000 schools districts they come from, demonstrate a specified competence in areas such as basic skills, science, AIDS and drug education, American history, and civics.

Chester Finn commenting on the 1989 Gallup poll results which revealed that the American public overwhelmingly supported national educational standards and a uniform national curriculum termed the results "A Seismic Shock for Education." "The hoariest policy assumption of American schooling—that essential decisions about curriculum and standards must be locally deter-mined—turns out to be another political myth." With words that echo a basic premise of this book, Finn suggests that ". . . it may be timely for elected officials to set aside the conservatism of the professionals and the incrementalism of the recent reform efforts and, instead, rewrite basic assumptions about how to chart the course and gauge the progress of the nation's schools."[6]

An explicit national policy that sets out the minimal educational and related requirements necessary to sustain the national interest can be translated into appropriate and relevant legislation. It is likely that a national policy achieved in this fashion, as contrasted with the current approach that employs extensive federal regula-tion and a threat of fiscal retaliation, in fact will allow more, rather than less, autonomy at the state, local, and school-building levels. For example, current federal programs targeted to the handicapped and the economically disadvantaged rely on extensive regulations and on a stultifying array of bureaucratic accountability measures. An explicit policy contained in appropriate legislation stating, at the most general level, what services the United States requires for its very young children, and what level of educational performance from its future adult citizens, could allow extraordinary flexibility and variety in the process of achieving these broadly stated goals. An authoritative, proactive role for the federal government does not imply a corresponding erosion of responsibility and authority at the state, local, or building level. For example, if a given state is convinced that its interests, as well as those of the United States, can best be secured by one form of teacher education rather than another or by a 210-day school year or by extraordinary delegation to the building level, it would be free to adopt such strategies. If a local school district prefers one curriculum, or school structure, over another, it would be free to exercise that prerogative as long as the strategies chosen in practice conform to state policies and will in effect satisfy the nation's explicitly delineated requirements.

Surely the time has come when a national educational policy must be formulated and implemented, a policy that can establish a minimal level of symmetry to replace the anarchy resulting from the uncoordinated actions of fifty states and 16,000 school boards. A national policy arrived at in a democratic manner and as an integral aspect of the nation's political process is preferable to policy formulated through the publicly unaccountable deliberations of a network of para-private institutions and categorical federal programs relying for their implementation on each of the fifty states deciding whether or not they will participate, on highly specific and detailed federal regulations, and on the ever-present threat of withdrawal of funding.

One sure thing about educational/youth policy is that the time line between implementation and results is problematically long. However, in a democracy, where political fortunes are determined every two, four, or six years, it is difficult to win needed support for often expensive policies that are targeted to secure results as much as a generation away. For example, even if the current child-care and educational policy processes are fundamentally restructured in the direction suggested here, it will be more than a decade before a resultant impact on the nation's youth would be realized. Conceivably a national policy dealing with prenatal, early childhood, and youth services put into place by the new administration might effectively permit the next generation of adolescents to escape the pathology that characterizes contemporary America's poor urban and rural youth. However, the massive, slow-moving educational/youth pipeline is a product of past as well as of current policy decisions. But the crisis is now; it impacts *today's* children and youth. Federal policy, therefore, must also take into account not only the needs of infants and children but the problems besieging contemporary youth as well. The alternatives suggested for consideration in Chapter 7 are directed to the immediate and critical problem posed by a growing population of disaffected poor and predominantly minority youth. Unless the national consequences of a growing, isolated, and predominantly minority permanent underclass are addressed, any contemplated national education/youth policy for millions of our young citizens may be too little but most certainly will be too late.

NOTES

1. "If Bush and Dukakis Really Care About Education . . . ,"
New York Times, 17 August 1988, I:23.

2. Ibid.

3. Samuel Halperin, "Some Diagnoses and Prescriptions," *Educational Policy in the Carter Years* (Washington, D.C.: George Washington University Press, 1978), 59.

4. "1987 Survey of Attitudes Towards Education," *Phi Delta Kappan*, 69 (September 1987): 17–30.

5. Chester E. Finn, "A Seismic Shock for Education," *New York Times*, 3 September 1989, E:13.

6. Ibid.

7

A National Youth Policy

YOUTH AT CRISIS

With few exceptions urban schools have failed to prepare nearly half of their inner-city youth either for jobs or for further education. The drop-out rate for most major city school systems hovers around the 50 percent mark. Nationally nearly one half of Hispanic students drop out of high school, yet by the year 2000 approximately 40 percent of the nation's public school students will consist of minority children and youth. If a situation wherein fewer than half of this rapidly growing, predominantly minority population either does not finish secondary school or is nonetheless unable to obtain meaningful employment or further education persists, then the nation is surely at serious risk.

In its 1987 report, *Children in Need*, the Committee for Economic Development, composed of many of the nation's major business leaders, warned: "This nation cannot continue to compete and prosper in the global arena, when more than one fifth of our children live in poverty and a third grow up in ignorance. . . . Allowing this to happen will not only impoverish these children but will impoverish our nation—culturally, politically and economically."[1]

The growing concentration and isolation of increasing numbers of minority youth in the urban ghettos and rural slums give powerful credence to the concept of a permanent underclass. Some scholars have gone a step further and suggest that what is in fact evolving is a uniquely American caste structure. "One of the more startling new theories holds that most blacks in America are in a social position strikingly similar to other 'castelike' minorities around the world." A global study of variations in performance on intelligence tests between minorities classified in caste terms and the majority population reveals a common pattern. Scholars who have studied this phenomenon believe that the lower "scores of children in these minorities . . . spring from factors such as prejudice. . . . In one pernicious form it becomes a self-fulfilling prophecy."[2]

Trapped in either urban or rural ghettos, many of today's minority youth have scant opportunity to comprehend or contemplate a future much different from that which describes their daily lives in their subculture. Therefore, for most poor minority youth, school, which has as its mission the inculcation of the mores and values of the dominant culture, is perceived as having only slight relevance to one's perceivable future. Worse still, school often serves as a persistent and humiliating reminder, at least by the standards of the dominant culture, that one is a failure. Education, which traditionally has been regarded as a primary vehicle for self-realization and for gainful employment, is increasingly perceived by many disadvantaged youth as an obstacle to getting on with their lives in their assigned universe. Thus, dropping out often becomes a way of salvaging one's self-esteem, or rejecting an increasingly alien and hostile culture for the relative security of a familiar milieu.

It is increasingly evident that a critical relationship exists between the growing racial discrepancy in standardized test scores and racial segregation and its attendant isolation and alienation. A recent study of the performance of high school students in New York City on the SATs not only reinforces the long-recognized discrepancy between the scores of black and Hispanic youngsters, on the one hand, and those of white and Asian youth, on the other, but also reveals the near exclusion of minority youngsters from the ranks of the upper-scoring population, as well as their preponderance in the lower levels. For example, whereas 10 percent of the white students scored above 650 on the math portion of the exam, only 1 percent of both the black and Hispanic youngsters did so; three times as many blacks and Hispanics as white students were likely to score under 300. A similar study by the University of Chicago on the relative performance of black/Hispanic and white students in Los Angeles reveals that the gap between the two groups is not narrowing but is in fact growing.[3]

The emerging subculture, empowered in recent years by the illicit drug industry, has spawned a host of well-organized and -armed urban "gangs" that in effect have taken control of certain neighborhoods in many of the nation's larger cities. Hardly a day goes by that one does not read of multiple killings of young predominantly black and Hispanic young men or of innocent children caught in a cross fire in pitched battles over turf and drugs. In Detroit, "shootings are so commonplace that they are the subject of local songs, and school essay contests. On the average, a child was shot every day in 1986."[4] Some 25 percent of Hispanic and 30 percent of black youth who die before reaching the age of nineteen are the victims of homicide.

Unemployment, violence, crime, and drug addiction and trafficking, along with school dropout, closely correlate with racial/class isolation and with the emergence of a permanent underclass and its attendant subculture. In New York City, for example, blacks, who constituted about 25 percent of the population in 1987, accounted for nearly 60 percent of the arrests for major felonies and nearly 70 percent of those for robbery.[5] However, attributing the recent national increase in violent crimes solely to the volatile interaction of "crack" and minority youth is deceptively simple. The current generation of predominantly minority inner-city and rural slum youth has come of age during a decade that has witnessed a significant curtailment of social welfare programs and is the beneficiary of a subtle but nonetheless comprehensible message that its plight is of relatively little concern to society at large. So crime solves both problems: It provides a substitute for the no-longer-available social welfare services, and it provides an opportunity to strike out against an unconcerned society. If this pathology is permitted to grow and fester, it has the capability of returning us to the endemic urban civil strife and violence of the 1960s. How soon we forget!

Today three of every four jobs require some education beyond secondary school. However, the likelihood of even the 50 percent of the inner-city students who do obtain a high school diploma finding work in the inner city or its immediate environs is not very great. The unemployment rate of black high school graduates, for example, is considerably higher than that of white high school dropouts. The changing nature of the economy has eliminated low-entry-level jobs that once abounded in the inner cities, whereas the few new job opportunities requiring relatively little education tend to be found in the service industry, and especially in the fast-food industry, nearly all of which are located in distant, essentially white segregated suburbs.[6]

Approximately half the nation's black teenagers are unemployed, and less than 7 percent hold full-time jobs. Even more indicative of the growing isolation and alienation that increasingly characterize this rapidly expanding sector of the nation's population is the fact that about 1.5 million black youth from the ages of sixteen to twenty-four have never held a job. Elijah Anderson, who has intensely studied the subject of black youth, concludes that "black inner-city youth unemployment constitutes an intractable social problem for the nation . . . tearing at the social and moral fabric of the society."[7]

A quarter century ago the employment/population ratio of black teenage males was higher than their white counterparts. Surely one cannot attribute this drastic falloff in urban black youth employment to what did or did not occur in the schools. However, there are those who would seek to resolve this issue by such school-based irrelevant strategies as a longer school year, higher standards, and more or less vocational training. The fact that there are essentially no jobs to be had regardless of the levels of educational attainment in the inner cities, and that an isolated, racially and class segregated subculture alienated from the mainstream has evolved, is neither a condition for which the schools can be blamed nor one that the schools can resolve.

The situation is getting progressively more serious. "Between 1973 and 1985 the mean incomes of all young men ages 20 to 24 declined 26.2%. Among blacks in the same age group, mean incomes fell 41.8%. . . . Among black high school graduates under age 20, only 49% were working, and of those only 45% were employed full time."[8]

It is endemic conditions such as these that contribute to low self-esteem, alienation, hostility, and a rejection of the cultural mainstream. Not surprisingly, the resultant self-image is often acted out in deliberate confrontation with majority mores and customs. This in turn gives credence to a white majority's assumption of pejorative racial differences, to growing racial prejudice and hostility, and increasingly to fear. The subculture's adoption of distinctive dress, language, and other mannerisms while effectively reinforcing a sense of pride and community exclusiveness also acts to isolate and alienate black youth further from the societal and economic mainstream. Pervasive unemployment and consequent isolation in the urban ghetto or rural slum, in conjunction with increasingly racially segregated schools, ensure the continued separation of young minority men and women from their counterparts in the "other culture."

Even when a minority youth does possess a high school diploma, and is also able to meet the required basic skill credentials required for a potential job, the subculture mannerisms and style frequently disincline potential employers from hiring even academically qualified minority youth. Such rejection tends to reinforce the distinctive style and provides little incentive to encourage minority youth to venture forth from the relative security of the ghetto. Furthermore, the underground illicit economy remains an attractive and lucrative, even if dangerous, option—an option that is likely to appear more attractive in the wake of rejection/failure by the "outside." In this fashion, petty (and not-so-petty) crime, an increasingly pervasive antiwork ethic, and a deliberate and overt rejection of majority white culture and society are perceived as proper and warranted. A major national study of the impending youth crisis concludes:

> If the unemployment situation continues with respect to black youth, the sense of failure and "outsidedness" will probably lead to increasing bitterness, hostility, and more alienation from American society. Crime and violence in the urban areas will rise as an increasingly angry and unruly black male population matures.[9]

The United States is not alone in facing a seemingly intractable problem of a growing and increasingly alienated minority youth. Technological changes transforming our society and economy are occurring throughout the industrialized Western world. We might be well advised to familiarize ourselves with comparable conditions abroad, for there is much that we could usefully learn. Ironically the United States, despite its long history of racial and ethnic conflict, has not responded as sensitively as have other Western democracies to the threats posed to national cohesion and tranquility by the evolution of a growing alienated and increasingly radicalized subculture.

Clearly a national youth policy for the rest of this century must take into consideration the educational and socialization requirements of this growing, increasingly disaffected and alienated population. Failure to address this crisis vigorously will guarantee a realization of the Kerner Commission warning of two decades ago, that this nation is "moving towards two societies, one black, one white—separate and unequal."[10]

FAILED RECORD OF FEDERAL YOUTH INITIATIVES

The conditions that characterize the lives of minority youth in the nation's large cities and rural slums were outlined in some detail to draw attention to the dimensions of the problem as well as to demonstrate that effective efforts at remediation will require more comprehensive and bold strategies than have been advanced by the barrage of national educational studies and their proposed reforms.

President Jimmy Carter's extensive efforts to reorganize the federal government analyzed the confusing and disjointed array of youth services provided by the various agencies of the federal government. His administration's commitment to establish a Department of Education provided an appropriate opportunity to consider the feasibility of aggregating many widely diffused youth and child services into a single new department. Proposals submitted to the president in 1977 suggested the establishment of a Department of Education and Human Development—certainly a move in the direction advanced here. A Department of Education and Human Development, it was thought, would subject the critical issues concerning education, children, and youth to the insights and expertise of a broader range of persons and thus provide a counterweight to the relatively narrow school/schooling perception of the dominant educational establishment.

The Carter task force proposed a sweeping restructuring of the federal government's responsibilities for child and youth services. Even though the Carter administration was sensitive to the magnitude and the national dimensions of the crisis afflicting the nation's children and youth, even to the point of seriously considering a radical restructuring of the government, it did not propose policy that would alter the traditional prohibition against a proactive role for the federal government in this area. Thus, the criteria selected to determine what would and what would not fall within the purview of the proposed Department of Education and Human Development were not based on a generic analysis of the targeted population and its needs but rather were determined by whether the services were perceived to be within the domain of state and local governments.

Despite its failure to consider a federal role in this area other than supplementing that of the states and localities, the Carter reorganization proposals, which would have gathered together within a single department most of the services affecting youth and children, are nonetheless significant. Although the reorganization attempts failed and gave way to more modest changes, they did have the effect of illuminating the holistic dimensions of the issue as well as establishing an important precedent. The situation that the Carter administration attempted, albeit unsuccessfully, to address is far more serious and pervasive today that it was then. Conceivably the magnitude and the imminence of the crisis will allow the new administration to pursue—hopefully with greater success—a comparably bold and imaginative approach in the 1990s.

It is more and more evident that schools and schooling, at least as presently constituted, are not equal to the task of reversing the cycle of ever-growing racial and class segregation, alienation, and radicalization. The schools have demonstrated that they are unable to educate and socialize a majority of inner-city and rural poor youth to a point that they are equipped either to enter the economic and cultural mainstream or to proceed to advanced education. We cannot escape the fact that by the year 2000 minority youngsters will constitute more than one third of the nation's public school students. It is critically important that we not lose sight of this demographic reality, for it is to this rapidly growing population of Americans that we must look for an increasing number of tomorrow's workers, scholars, and soldiers as well as for our political and cultural leaders. If current policies persist, fewer than one half of this critically important population will finish secondary school. Most will likely remain trapped in increasingly lawless urban ghettos and rural slums. Fewer and fewer minority urban and poor rural youth will escape the stultifying limitations of their subcultures either through higher education or gainful employment. The catastrophic implications for the future of the United States if the status quo persists as the agenda for the future are painfully evident.

Federal youth programs, other than those related directly to schools and schooling, with few exceptions, historically were administered by agencies other than the U.S. Office of Education. Long-standing concerns over turf, issues of local control, and constitutionality inclined Washington policymakers, when dealing with youth issues, to avoid the office and subsequently the Department of Education and to turn instead to other federal agencies such as the Departments of Labor, Health, and Agriculture. The absence of a major governmental agency charged with primary responsibility for youth services tended to relegate these concerns to a secondary and derivative status, with the result that youth policy is likely addressed only in response to other seemingly more critical concerns such as national security, unemployment, or civil strife. However, the youth problem facing the nation today is less a derivative of more profound national concerns than it is a generic issue in its own right. The sporadic, episodic, and diffuse nature of policy in this vital area is partly attributable to a persistent failure, or disinclination, to address the issue in a holistic, comprehensive manner.

The policy landscape is littered with the remains of relatively short-lived federal programs mounted to resolve ill-defined problems of a little understood population. It is neither feasible nor desirable to attempt to catalog the dozens of national youth initiatives that have come and gone since the New Deal era. Most have been multifaceted, others have been conflicting and confusing, and rarely were they accompanied by an effective evaluation process. The policy goals often have not been clearly articulated, typically combining an intent simultaneously to increase employability, change the distribution of income, solve issues of social conflict, reduce crime, lower the premarital teenage birthrate, and so on.

Available data suggest that most federal youth programs have done little to alleviate youth unemployment, to incline youngsters to remain in or to return to school, or enhance their employability significantly. As long as national youth policy remains diffusely spread over a host of unrelated agencies, it is likely that the current confusion and absence of focus and meaningful evaluation will persist.

In short, neither schools nor youth employment and related policies have proved effective in arresting the cycle of alienation and radicalization that characterizes a growing number of inner-city and rural poor, predominantly minority youth. This is attributable not only to the diffuse and chaotic nature of the federal programs but also to the fact that they are perceived by their intended beneficiaries as an alien intrusion and thus essentially irrelevant or at best marginal to life in the segregated subculture. The underlying assumption of federal youth policies is that the various programs, in one way or another, will acquaint urban youth with mainstream values and behavior. However, this assumption fails to take into consideration the likelihood that the intended message is not perceived by many as particularly relevant to survival in their isolated subculture. Thus, it is not surprising that the only substantive programs that have proved relatively effective are those that act to physically remove minority urban and rural poor youth from their isolated environments. The military, for example, has probably done more to orient troubled youth toward the societal and economic mainstream than the entire array of federal youth programs. In recent years, however, the military increasingly has been able to fill its ranks with high school graduates. In the past five years more than 90 percent of the enlistees in the armed forces had a high school diploma, with the result that even this avenue of escape for many of the nation's disadvantaged youth has been effectively cut off.

The federal programs directed to youth training/education and employment with few exceptions have tended to be small in scale and have impacted relatively little on the potential clientele. Most have targeted the urban and rural poor and particularly those who have dropped out or who seem prone to drop out of school. The programs vary as to the targeted population, the duration of the training/educational experience, and the mix of experiential, vocational, and academic components. However, the myriad of overlapping federal programs have not effectively addressed the fundamental issues that lie at the heart of the urban minority youth crisis.

The Job Training Partnership Act (JTPA), which replaced the Comprehensive Employment and Training Act (CETA) in 1982, is currently the major federal nonresidential youth program and serves about one-half million young people, about 5 percent of those eligible.[11] The act requires that at least 40 percent of the funds appropriated be dedicated to servicing the needs of disadvantaged youth. JTPA programs are designed, implemented, and managed by private industry councils composed of local businesspeople as well as representatives of community civic organizations. The states and localities are left to determine pretty much on their own how and for what they will expend their federal funds. Unlike CETA, JTPA programs do not pay participating youth a stipend to keep them enrolled; nor does JTPA incorporate an intensive work component. In contrast to CETA, JTPA programs are more inclined to include a heavy concentration of basic skills remediation. In 1986 JTPA programs enrolled nearly 300,000 in classroom training programs, of which 41 percent were youth under twenty-two years of age.[12] For these reasons JTPA programs have been assessed primarily on the extent of successful job placement and on skill and academic performance standards. Unfortunately this has inclined those responsible for the JTPA programs to "cream off" those youth possessed of attributes that tend to ensure relatively quick and easy success, with the result that the intended target population of drop- or dropping-out youth receives short shrift. In 1985 JTPA served a total of 462,848 young people. However, only 90,000 of these were high school dropouts.[13] Only about one third of the total enrolled in that year subsequently entered employment. A Labor Department audit in 1988 found that JTPA tended to target easy-to-place trainees and also noted that about 50 percent of those enrolled were still unemployed after their training had been completed.[14]

Although available data are not always consistent or comprehensive, experience to date suggests that programs that employ part-time work as an inducement to return dropouts to school are not very effective. In the long run the tendency to mount programs of a short duration at correspondingly low cost is particularly ineffective. Occupational training programs that give the appearance of success, as measured by such criteria as job placement, employability, academic remediation, and earnings, usually contain a strong academic remedial component, are of relatively long duration, and relocate the participating youth, for at least part of the time, from his or her pervasive subcultural environment.

It is generally agreed that to date the Job Corps has proved to be the most successful federally funded youth intervention program. Although extraordinary variety characterizes the management and programs of the nation's 107 Job Corps centers located in forty-one states, they all have demonstrated a record of relative success. Job Corps centers share two important attributes that distinguish them from nearly all other federal youth initiatives. They are residential, and they mount programs of relatively long duration. While commissioner of education in New Jersey this writer was responsible for one of the nation's largest Job Corps centers and had an extensive firsthand opportunity to become familiar with both the advantages and liabilities of this approach to the youth problem. As policymakers design the next generation of programs for disadvantaged youth, they might well familiarize themselves with the variable experience of the Job Corps.

Enrollment in the Job Corps is voluntary. However, in reality a number of young men and women who have had to appear in court on minor charges are "encouraged" to enroll in a Job Corps center rather than face the likelihood of incarceration. A federal youth policy might seek to develop programs that facilitate and legitimize this process.

Employment placement and retention records of the Job Corps centers average more than 80 percent. Unfortunately at a given time the nation's 107 Job Corps centers are capable of enrolling only about 41,000 youth—a tiny fraction of those in need. Obviously a residential program of this duration and quality is relatively expensive. The average yearly per participant cost in 1986 was approximately $6,000, significantly less, however, than what is required to support a student in a college or university. If it is in the national interest to provide public funding to ensure an opportunity for all academically eligible young Americans to attend a college or university, does it not follow that the national interest would be equally well served if a comparable level of assistance were made available to support the education and training needs of our disadvantaged urban and rural youth?

ELEMENTS OF AN ALTERNATIVE
NATIONAL YOUTH POLICY

It is increasingly evident that the existing national youth and child policy—or more precisely, nonpolicy—advocating a marginal restructuring of schools and schooling and a grab bag of short-lived youth training programs is not about to arrest the nation's accelerating drift toward the institutionalization of a dissident, alienated, and potentially radicalized predominantly minority subculture in its inner cities and rural slums. Urgently required is a national policy that focuses on this population as its primary target and concern. The obvious national interests at stake and the escalating magnitude and catastrophic implications of the youth problem are such that a policy of campaign rhetoric and episodic supplementing of local and state initiatives will not suffice. A Department of Youth and Child Services ideally would include legislated authority and a corresponding administrative capability to attack this problem in a comprehensive fashion. This is not to suggest that it do so to the exclusion of private, state, and local government agencies. As outlined above, what is suggested is that the truly national dimensions of the issue be delineated and authoritatively promulgated. An expanded role for the federal government does not have to be obtained at the expense of a dilution of state, local, or community authority. Precisely enunciated federal policy can provide the parameters within which other participating agencies function. Failure to accommodate the requirements inherent in the federal statutes would thus be an issue for the courts to adjudicate—unlike the current situation wherein federal funds, diffusely allocated, are made available or withheld according to a bureaucratic judgment as to whether regulations have been met.

If one accepts the position that the nation's growing population of disadvantaged, mostly minority youth, given existing diffuse, decentralized, and tangential policies, cannot be assimilated into the economic and social mainstream, then the development of an appropriate national youth policy is not only appropriate but imperative. If one accepts the argument that the nation's segregated, isolated urban ghettos and rural slums are spawning an increasingly violent and radicalized subculture, a threat to the nation's very future, then policies that attempt to provide an opportunity for millions of American youth trapped in this quagmire to experience an alternative life, and in the process an opportunity to become a part of the greater society, are of paramount national interest!

Although it is neither possible nor appropriate to attempt to develop relevant strategies in this book, some general aspects of an alternative policy can be attempted. Consideration might be given to distinguishing more precisely between the needs of adolescents and those of other school-age children. Schools and schooling essentially do, or likely can, meet the requirements of most preadolescent children, even in the nation's inner cities. The near obsession of the many reform studies and proposals with secondary schooling reflects an understanding that the crisis is primarily one afflicting adolescents and young adults. Some thought might usefully be given to uncoupling the current governance and/or administrative association of primary and secondary schooling, at least under certain circumstances. It is useful to recall that the existing governance structure of linking the management of primary and secondary education within the same system was not always the rule.

Conceivably services for adolescents, including education, might be more effectively managed by a system that has as its major concern the holistic needs of this unique population, rather than being limited to their narrow educational requirements. Some thought might be devoted to examining the possible advantages of linking adolescent and other youth services, including education, with the nation's system of community colleges. Or it might be desirable to contemplate the development of new representative local and community governance structures that would involve institutions and individuals concerned with and knowledgeable about the entire array of youth needs. Recently the citizens of Dade County, Florida, voted to establish a separate governance unit, replete with its own authority to levy taxes to administer an entire range of services to children and youth. Five members of the proposed nine-member governing board would be appointed by the governor. The remainder include a county commissioner, the school superintendent, the head of the local state welfare agency, and a school board member.

As controversial as it may seem at first glance, the magnitude of the crisis is such that it may be necessary to consider the wisdom of incorporating within this system authority, under certain circumstances, to prescribe the substance as well as the location of youth education and training programs, including, for example, enrollment and/or assignment in institutions such as Job Corps centers. Nearly every state has a Job Corps center in place and conceivably could, with federal government assistance, expand its capability to reach a much larger population. Given the seemingly intractable and pervasive influence of the inner-city and rural slum environments, it is doubtful whether any youth program mounted in such a milieu will significantly and positively affect the long-time life chances of a substantial portion of these young Americans. If this is indeed the case then it is necessary to contemplate a substantially massive program, drawing from Job Corps and other relevant experience, to provide such an opportunity. Some Job Corps centers are effectively located on former military bases. Consideration might be given to a more systematic analysis of the availability and utility of vacant or to-be-vacated military facilities as well as to the possibility of incorporating alternative youth programs alongside and possibly even as a part of the basic training component of existing military bases. A policy to expand Job Corps centers utilizing military facilities slated for closing might prove politically feasible, for it would at the same time address the imminent youth crisis and rescue the threatened local economies. Conceivably the federal government might transfer ownership of the facilities along with a formula-based shared program cost to the states with the stipulation that Job Corps centers be established.

The United States is one of the few industrialized nations that does not require compulsory national service. Some consideration might be given to restructuring and rethinking "national service." In 1988/89, however, the subject of youth service began to attract considerable attention at both the state and national levels.

During the 1988 presidential campaign, Vice President Bush promised when elected to establish a national foundation that would promote a domestic youth corps: YES—Youth Engaged in Service to America. State political leaders have also expressed interest in some form of youth service. A California law passed in 1988, for example, encourages and facilitates volunteer service on the part of the state's 400,000 undergraduate students enrolled in public institutions of higher education. Maryland is the first state to require a degree of youth service.

At the federal level, Senator Sam Nunn has been the major advocate of a voluntary national youth service program. His proposed legislation would require all recipients of federal student financial aid to perform two years of national service. A two-year hitch, which could be either of a military or civilian nature, would enable a national volunteer to accumulate "national service vouchers" exchangeable for up to $12,000 of educational or housing benefits. The scheme envisaged recruiting some 700,000 volunteers. The Nunn proposals have generated considerable opposition, particularly from the higher education community, fearing that program funding would come from existing student financial programs that currently reach some 2 million first-year college students. Other members of Congress have also introduced legislation. It seems likely that some form of voluntary national youth service legislation, probably not tied to student financial aid, will find its way through Congress in the next few years. Whether such legislation will effectively encourage and reward inner-city and poor rural youth to break out of the ghetto and find their way into the mainstream of society is still to be seen.

Thought might at some point, be given to requiring some form of national service for all young American men and women. This writer's involuntary experience in the military during two wars and long association with the Peace Corps strongly suggest that such experiences could significantly breach the growing barriers problematically separating increasingly isolated American youth subcultures.

Our failure, from a policy point of view, to distinguish the unique needs of the nation's adolescents and young adults has inclined us to lump them together with either children or adults. The vexing persistent problems posed by the nation's juvenile justice system are indicative of this failure to delineate sensitively the needs of this unique and often troubled population. The Bush administration might consider a comprehensive study of the nation's juvenile justice systems. It is conceivable that such a study might find merit in the development of a system of adjudication and counseling for youth separate and distinct from the existing criminal justice system—one that might incorporate functions such as personal as well as job counseling, alternative educational and other youth service assignments, and coordination of relevant youth services.

This summary history of national youth policies and brief outline of a few alternatives are not designed to be comprehensive but merely illustrative. The purposes of this analysis are to document the ineffectiveness of piecemeal federal programs and the nature and dimensions of the national youth crisis and to suggest that more audacious and comprehensive approaches will be required if the nation is to avert an impending apocalypse.

The school and schooling studies and accompanying reform proposals of the 1980s have acted to obscure the more fundamental issues of youth and children in crisis. The proposed reforms are directed to the attention of the nation's 16,000 relatively autonomous school boards and fifty state governments. To expect that this near state of educational anarchy will somehow steep itself in the myriad of reform proposals and in a miraculous fashion systematically aggregate hundreds of thousands of parochial decisions into an effective uniform national educational policy capable of addressing a national youth and child crisis is a most dangerous denial of reality. Required is an alternative policy-making process that will provide for an authoritative policy role for the national government while maintaining and even enhancing the involvement of educational and other professionals, local citizenry, parents, and state governments.

The illustrative alternative strategies briefly outlined here are certainly not definitive. But they are suggestive of the kinds of solutions that might be forthcoming if questions more comprehensive than those limited to school and schooling are posed more frequently.

The national interest requires that the new administration provide the leadership required to restructure critical aspects of the country's educational and other child and youth services. It is increasingly evident that there does indeed exist a clear and present child and youth crisis in the United States—a crisis with the potential for a national catastrophe.

NOTES

1. Committee for Economic Development, Research and Policy Committee, *Children in Need: Investment Strategies for the Educationally Disadvantaged* (New York: Committee for Economic Development, 1987), 1.

2. Daniel Goleman, "Black Child's Self-View Is Still Low, Study Finds," *New York Times*, 31 August 1987, I:13.

3. Lee A. Daniels, "Race and School Achievement Are Examined," *New York Times*, 25 October 1987, I:22.

4. Isabel Wilkerson, "Detroit Crime Feeds on Itself and Youth," *New York Times*, 29 April 1987, I:1.

5. Sam Roberts, "Race and Crime: Beyond Statistics to Find Answers," *New York Times*, 16 November 1987, II:1.

6. Despite the evolution in recent years of a substantial minority middle class and despite its exodus from the inner city, America's suburbs are still predominantly white. Blacks make up only 7 to 9 percent of the population of the nation's suburbs.

7. Elijah Anderson, "Some Observations of Black Youth Un-

employment," *Youth Employment and Public Policy* (Englewood Cliffs, N.J.: Prentice-Hall, 1980), 64.

8. William T. Grant Foundation Commission on Work, Family and Citizenship, *The Forgotten Half: Non-College Youth in America* (Washington, D.C.: William T. Grant Foundation, 1988), 16.

9. Ibid., 86.

10. Governor Otto Kerner, National Advisory Commission on Civil Disorders, 1968.

11. William T. Grant Foundation Commission on Work, Family and Citizenship, *The Forgotten Half*, 7.

12. William T. Grant Foundation Commission on Work, Family and Citizenship, *Current Federal Policies and Programs for Youth* (Washington, D.C.: J. R. Reingold Associates, 1987), 5.

13. Ibid., 6.

14. *Christian Science Monitor*, 19 November 1988, 3.

Selected Bibliography

Adler, Mortimer J. *The Paideia Proposal*. New York: Macmillan, 1982.

Altbach, Philip G., ed. *Excellence in Education: Perspectives on Policy and Practice*. Buffalo, N.Y.: Prometheus Books, 1985.

Anderson, Elijah. "Some Observations of Black Youth Unemployment." *Youth Employment and Public Policy*. Englewood Cliffs, N.J.: Prentice-Hall, 1980.

Andrig, Gregory R. "Education Standards, Testing, and Equity." *Phil Delta Kappan* 66:9 (May 1985): 623–25.

————. "Teacher Education and Teacher Testing: The Rush to Mandate." *Phi Delta Kappan* 67:6 (February 1986): 447–51.

Auletta, Ken. *The Underclass*. New York: Random House, 1982.

Bailey, Stephen K. *Education Interest Groups in the Nation's Capital*. Washington, D.C.: American Council on Education, 1975.

Beckwith, Bill E., et al. "Vasopressin Analog (DDAVP) Facilitates Conceptual Learning in Human Males." *Peptides* 3:4 (1982): 628.

Bell, Terrel H. "Education Policy Development in the Reagan Administration." *Phi Delta Kappan* 67:7 (March 1986): 488–93.

Berke, Joel, and Michael Kirst. *Federal Aid to Education.* Lexington, Mass.: D. C. Heath, 1972.

Berke, Richard L. "Bush's Domestic Policy Team Is All Set, But Not the Agenda." *New York Times*, 18 January 1989, I:1.

————. "Capital Offers a Ripe Market to Drug Dealers." *New York Times*, 28 March 1989, I:16.

Bernstein, Richard. "20 Years after the Kerner Report: Three Societies, All Separate." *New York Times*, 29 February 1988, I:8.

Bickel, Robert. "Educational Reform and the Equivalence of Schools." *Issues in Education* 4:3 (Winter 1986): 179–97.

Bickel, Robert, and Martha J. Chang. "Public Schools, Private Schools and the Common School Ideal." *Urban Review* 17:2 (1985): 75–97.

Biebel, Charles. "Private Foundations and Public Policy: The Case of Secondary Education during the Great Depression." *History of Education Quarterly* (Spring 1976).

Boyd, William. "The Public, the Professionals, and Educational Policy-making: Who Governs?" *Teacher College Record* 77 (1976).

Boyer, Ernest L. *High School: A Report on Secondary Education in America.* New York: Harper & Row, 1983.

Brown, Rexford. *Reconnecting Youth: The Next Stage of Reform: A Report from the Business Advisory Commission.* Denver: Education Commission of the States, 1985.

Bruder, Leonard. "Decentralization of Schools Provides Painful Lessons." *New York Times*, 11 December 1988, IV:6.

Carnegie Foundation for the Advancement of Teaching, Board of Trustees. *An Imperiled Generation: Saving Urban Schools.* Princeton, N.J.: Princeton University Press, 1988.

Children's Defense Fund. *A Call for Action to Make Our Nation Safe for Children: A Briefing Book on the States of Amer-*

ican Children. Washington, D.C.: Children's Defense Fund, 1988.

Chubb, John. "To Revive Schools, Dump Bureaucrats." *New York Times*, 9 December 1988, I:35.

Cohen, David K. "Policy and Organization: The Impact of State and Federal Educational Policy on School Governance." *Harvard Educational Review* 52:4 (November 1982): 486.

Coleman, James S. "Public Schools, Private Schools, and the Public Interest." *American Education* 18 (January-February 1982): 17–22.

Committee for Economic Development, Research and Policy Committee. *Investing In Our Children: Business and the Public Schools*. New York: Committee for Economic Development, 1985.

———. *Children in Need: Investment Strategies for the Educationally Disadvantaged*. New York: Committee for Economic Development, 1987.

Conant, James Bryant. *Shaping Educational Policy*. New York: McGraw-Hill, 1964.

———. "Proposal for a Nation Wide Educational Policy." Reprint, February 1965, *Education Digest* 57 (November 1985).

Coons, John E., and Stephan D. Sugarman. *Education by Choice: The Case for Family Control*. Berkeley: University of California Press, 1978.

Cremins, Lawrence. *The Republic and the School*. New York: Teacher College Press, 1957.

Cuomo, Mario. "State of the State Address." *New York Times*, 7 January 1988, I:1.

———. "Excerpts from Governor's Budget Message to the Legislature: Cuomo Asks Increases for Education and Housing." *New York Times*, 14 January 1988, II:5.

Daniels, Lee A. "Race and School Achievement Are Examined." *New York Times*, 25 October 1987, I:22.

Danziger, Sheldon H., and Daniel H. Weinberg, eds. *Fighting*

Poverty: What Works and What Doesn't. Cambridge: Harvard University Press, 1986.

DeYoung, Alan J. *Economics and American Education.* White Plains, N.Y.: Longman, 1989.

Down, Graham. "Assassins of Excellence." In *The Great School Debate: Which Way for American Education?*, ed. Beatrice Gross and Ronald Gross. New York: Simon and Schuster, 1985.

Doyle, Denis P. "Your Meager Slice of New Federalism Could Contain Delicious Options for Schools." *American School Board Journal* 169:4 (April 1982): 23–25.

———. *From Theory to Practice: Considerations for Implementing a Statewide Voucher System.* Sacramento, Calif.: Sequoia Institute, 1984.

Doyle, Denis P. and Chester E. Finn, Jr. "American Schools and the Future of Local Control." *Public Interest* 77 (Fall 1984): 77–95.

Education Commission of the States. *A Summary of Major Reports on Education.* Denver: Education Commission of the States, 1983.

Education Commission of the States, Task Force on Education for Economic Growth. *Action for Excellence: A Comprehensive Plan to Improve Our Nation's Schools.* Denver: Education Commission of the States, 1983.

———. *Action in the States: Progress toward Education Renewal.* Denver: Education Commission of the States, 1984.

Everhart, Robert, ed. *The Public School Monopoly: A Critical Analysis of Education and the State in American Society.* Cambridge: Ballinger, 1982.

Feagin, Joe R. "Changing Black Americans to Fit a Racist System?" *Journal of Social Issues* 43:1 (1987): 85–89.

Finn, Chester E., Jr. "Reflections on 'The Disassembly of the Federal Educational Role.'" *Education and Urban Society* 15:3 (May 1983): 389–96.

Fiske, Edward. "Hispanic Pupils' Plight Cited in Study." *New York Times*, 26 July 1987, I:24.

———. "U.S. Testing of Students Raises Growing Debate." *New York Times*, 27 December 1987, I:28.

Franklin, Jon. *Molecules of the Mind: The Brave New Science of Molecular Psychology.* New York: Atheneum, 1987.

Garms, Walter, James Gutherie, and Lawrence Pierce. *School Finance: The Economics and Politics of Federalism.* Englewood Cliffs, N.J.: Prentice-Hall, 1978.

Goleman, Daniel. "Black Child's Self-View Is Still Low, Study Finds." *New York Times*, 31 August 1987, I:13.

Goodlad, John I. *A Place Called School: Prospects for the Future.* New York: McGraw-Hill, 1983.

Gove, Samuel K., and Frederick M. Wirt, eds. *Political Science and School Politics.* Lexington, Mass.: Lexington Books, 1976.

Graham, Hugh Davis. *The Uncertain Triumph: Federal Education Policy in the Kennedy and Johnson Years.* Chapel Hill: University of North Carolina Press, 1984.

Green, Joslyn. *Conversations: 20 Years in American Education.* Denver: Education Commission of the States, 1985.

Gross, Beatrice, and Ronald Gross, eds. *The Great School Debate: Which Way for American Education?* New York: Simon and Schuster, 1985.

Gutherie, James, ed. *School Finance Policies and Practices.* Cambridge: Ballinger, 1980.

Halperin, Samuel. "Some Diagnoses and Prescriptions." *Educational Policy in the Carter Years.* Washington, D.C.: George Washington University Press, 1978.

Harshman, Richard; Elizabeth Hampson; and Sheri A. Berenbaum. "Individual Differences in Cognitive Abilities and Brain Organization, Part 1. Sex and Handedness Differences in Ability." *Canadian Journal of Psychology* 37:1 (March 1983): 144–92.

Havighurst, Robert. "Philanthropic Foundations as Interest Groups." *Education and Urban Society* 13:2 (1981): 193–218.

Hechinger, Fred M. "87's Mixed Report Card." *New York Times*, 29 December 1987, III:11.

Hevesi, Dennis. "Board Named to Set Teacher Standards." *New York Times*, 16 May 1987, I:9.

Heyns, Roger W. "Education and Society: A Complex Interaction." *American Education* 20 (May 1984): 2–5.

Hodgkin, Harold. *All One System: Demographics of Education, Kindergarten through Graduate School.* Washington, D.C.: Institute for Educational Leadership, 1985.

———. "Changing Society, Unchanging Curriculum." *National Forum: Phi Kappa Phi Journal* 67:3 (Summer 1987): 8–11.

———. "Courage to Change: Facing Our Demographic Destiny." *Currents* 13:7 (July-August 1987): 8–12.

Honig, Bill. *Last Chance for Our Children: How You Can Help Save Our Schools.* Indianapolis, Ind. Addison-Wesley, 1985.

———. "The Educational Excellence Movement: Now Comes the Hard Part." *Phi Delta Kappan* 66:10 (June 1985): 675–81.

Howe, Harold III. "National Politics and the Schools." *Change* 15 (July-August 1983).

———. "Education Moves to Center Stage: An Overview of Recent Studies." *Phi Delta Kappan* 65:3 (November 1983): 167–72.

———. "Symposium on the Year of the Reports: Responses from the Educational Community." *Harvard Educational Review* 54:1 (February 1984): 1–31.

———. "The Prospect for Children in the United States." *Phi Delta Kappan* 68:4 (November 1986): 191–96.

Institute for Educational Leadership. *School Boards: Strengthening Grass Roots Leadership.* Washington, D.C.: Institute for Educational Leadership, 1986.

Johnson, Dirk. "Companies Create 'Model School' for Urban Poor." *New York Times*, 26 October 1988, II:10.

Johnson, Julie. "Schools Faulted on Educating Blacks." *New York Times*, 24 May 1989, II:8.

Katz, Michael B. *The Irony of Early School Reform*. Boston: Beacon Press, 1968.

————. *Class, Bureaucracy and Schools: The Illusion of Educational Change in America*. New York: Praeger, 1975.

Kennedy, E. M. "Government and Education: Who Is Responsible?" *Education Digest* 49 (May 1984).

Keppel, Francis. "A Field Guide to the Land of Teachers." *Phi Delta Kappan* 68:1 (September 1986): 18–23.

Kerr, Peter. "Rich vs. Poor: Drug Patterns Are Diverging." *New York Times*, 30 August 1987, I:28.

Kirst, Michael W. *State, School, and Politics: Research Directions*. Lexington, Mass.: D. C. Heath, 1972.

————. "Sustaining the Momentum of State Education Reform: The Link between Assessment and Financial Support." *Phi Delta Kappan* 67:5 (January 1986): 341–45.

Koener, James. *Who Controls American Education?* Boston: Beacon Press, 1968.

Lagemann, Ellen C. *Private Power for the Public Good*. Middletown, Conn.: Wesleyan University Press, 1983.

Leman, Nicholas. "The Unfinished War." *Atlantic* 262:6 (December 1988): 46.

Levine, Donald, and Mary Jo Bane. *The Inequality Controversy: Schooling and Distributive Justice*. New York: Basic Books, 1975.

Lewis, Neil A. "School Boards Found Failing to Meet Goals." *New York Times*, 5 December 1988, II:1.

Liberman, Myron. *Beyond Public Education*. New York: Praeger, 1986.

Merleman, Richard. "Democratic Politics and the Culture of American Education." *American Political Science Review* 74 (1980): 320.

Morgan, Thomas. "U.S. Schools Are Said to Fail in Reducing Bias." *New York Times*, 3 May 1987, I:55.

Moynihan, Daniel Patrick. *Beyond the Melting Pot: The Negroes,*

Puerto Ricans, Jews, Italians, and Irish of New York City. Cambridge: MIT Press, 1963.

———. "The New Science of Politics." *Public Interest* 86 (Winter 1987): 22–35.

Myrdal, Gunnar. *An American Dilemma.* New York: Harper & Row, 1969.

National Commission on Excellence in Education. *A Nation at Risk: The Imperative for Educational Reform.* Washington, D.C.: Government Printing Office, 1983.

National Science Board Commission on Precollege Education in Mathematics, Science and Technology. *Educating Americans for the 21st Century.* Washington, D.C.: National Science Foundation, 1983.

Ornstein, A. C. "The Changing Federal Role in Education." *American Education* 20 (December 1984): 4–7.

Perkinson, Henry J. *200 Years of American Educational Thought.* New York: University Printers of America, 1976.

Perlez, Jane. "The Debate on Schools—Educators Say Thrust of Cuomo Proposals Doesn't Address the Needs of Schoolhouse." *New York Times,* 12 December 1987, I:35.

Peterson, Paul. *Making the Grade: Report of the Twentieth Century Fund Task Force on Federal Elementary and Secondary Education Policy.* New York: Priority Press Publications, 1983.

Pettigrew, Thomas, and Joanne Martin. "Shaping the Organizational Context for Black American Inclusion." *Journal of Social Issues* 43:1 (1987): 41–78.

Pifer, Alan. "The Social Role of Government in a Free Enterprise System." *Integrated Education* 19:3–6 (May-December 1981): 2–8.

Powell, Arthur G., Eleanor Farrar, and David K. Cohen. *The Shopping Mall High School: Winners and Losers in the Educational Marketplace.* Boston: Houghton Mifflin, 1985.

Ravitch, Diane. *The Troubled Crusade: American Education 1945–1980.* New York: Basic Books, 1983.

———. "On Thinking About the Future." *Phi Delta Kappan* 64:5 (January 1983): 317–20.

———. "The Continuing Crisis: Fashions in Education." *American Scholar* 53:2 (Spring 1984): 183–93.

———. *The Schools We Deserve.* New York: Basic Books, 1985.

Reiser, Morton F. *Mind, Brain, Body: Toward Convergence of Psychoanalysis and Neurobiology.* New York: Basic Books, 1984.

Resnick, Lauren. "The Presidential Address: Learning in School and Out." *Educational Researcher* 16:9 (December 1987): 13–20.

Roberts, Sam. "The Race Factor: Do Educators See Differences?" *New York Times*, 16 November 1987, II:1.

Rosenholtz, Susan J. "Political Myths about Educational Reform: Lessons from Research on Teaching." *Phi Delta Kappan* 66:5 (January 1985): 349–55.

Rosenthal, Allen, ed. *Governing American Education: A Reader on Politics, Power, and Public School Policy.* Garden City, N.Y.: Doubleday, 1969.

Sandman, Curt, et al. "Are Learning and Attention Related to the Sequence of Amino-Acids in ACTH-MSH Peptides?" *Peptides* 1:4 (1980): 280.

Schmidt, William E. "High AIDS Rate Spurring Efforts for Minorities." *New York Times*, 2 August 1987, I:1.

Shanker, Albert. "Our Profession, Our Schools: The Case for Fundamental Reform." *American Educator* 10:3 (Fall 1986): 44–45.

———. "Convention Plots New Course." *New York Times*, 10 July 1988, IV:7.

Sizer, Theodore R. *Horace's Compromise: The Dilemma of the American High School.* Boston: Houghton Mifflin, 1984.

———. "A Vote for 'Messiness.'" *Phi Delta Kappan* 67:2 (October 1985): 125–26.

Solorzano, Lucia. "Teaching in Trouble." *U.S. News & World Report* 100:20 (26 May 1986): 52–57.

Spring, Joel. "Education and the SONY Wars." *Phi Delta Kappan* 65:8 (April 1984): 534–37.

————. *American Education: An Introduction to Social and Political Aspects*. White Plains, N.Y.: Longman, 1985.

————. *Conflict of Interest: The Politics of American Education*. White Plains, N.Y.: Longman, 1988.

————. *The Sorting Machine Revisited: National Educational Policy since 1945*. White Plains, N.Y.: Longman, 1989.

Steadman, Lawrence C., and Marshall S. Smith. "Weak Arguments, Poor Data, Simplistic Recommendations." In *The Great School Debate: Which Way for American Education?*, ed. Beatrice Gross and Ronald Gross, 83–105. New York: Simon and Schuster, 1985.

Sullivan, Joseph F. "Program to Aid Troubled Youths: Jersey Schools Will Offer Counseling on Drug Abuse and Family Problems." *New York Times*, 10 January 1988, I:27.

Suro, Roberto. "John Paul Assails Economic Plight of Blacks in U.S." *New York Times*, 13 September 1987, I:1.

Thatcher, R. W., et al. "Effects of Low Levels of Cadmium and Lead on Cognitive Functioning in Children." *Archives of Environmental Health* 37:3 (May-June 1982): 164.

Timpane, Michael, ed. *The Federal Interest in Financing Education*. Cambridge: Ballinger, 1979.

Tucker, Marc. "The Carnegie Report—A Call for Redesigning the Schools." *Phi Delta Kappan* 68:1 (September 1986): 24–27.

U.S. Commission on Civil Rights. *Desegregation of the Nation's Schools: A Status Report*. Washington, D.C.: Government Printing Office, 1979.

Vance, Victor S., and Philip C. Schlechty. *The Structure of the Teaching Occupation and the Characteristics of Teachers*. Washington, D.C.: National Institute of Education 81-0100, 1981.

Wilkerson, Isabel. "Detroit Crime Feeds on Itself and Youth." *New York Times*, 29 April 1987, I:1.

William T. Grant Foundation Commission on Work, Family and

Citizenship. *Current Federal Policies and Programs for Youth.* Washington, D.C.: J. R. Reingold Associations, 1987.

———. *The Forgotten Half: Non-College-Bound Youth in America.* Washington, D.C.: William T. Grant Foundation, 1988.

Wilson, William Julius. *The Inner City and Public Policy.* Chicago: Chicago University Press, 1987.

Wirt, Frederick M., and Michael W. Kirst. *Schools in Conflict.* Berkeley: McCutchan Publishing Corp., 1982.

Wise, Arthur E. *Legislated Learning: The Bureaucratization of the American Classroom.* Berkeley: University of California Press, 1979.

Woodside, William S. "The Corporate Role in Public Education." *Social Policy* 15:2 (Fall 1984): 44–45.

Index

ABOUT THE AUTHOR

FRED G. BURKE has been involved with and in American education for thirty years. He received his B.A. from Williams College. He earned his M.A. and Ph.D. in Political Science from Princeton in 1958, where he was a National Woodrow Wilson Fellow and was also awarded the Sanaxy Fellowship in Practical Ethics. His doctoral dissertation received the Kimborough Owen Award of the American Political Science Association.

Dr. Burke's career has been divided between an interest in international affairs and American public education. He has written a number of books on international affairs, primarily concerned with Africa. Since 1960 he has been actively involved in American public education, first as Rhode Island's Commissioner of Education and from 1974 to 1982 as New Jersey's Commissioner of Education. He is currently Professor of Political Science at the University of Connecticut, where he teaches and writes on public policy issues affecting education, and he has served on many national committees, boards, and task forces.